Shattering Truths

I Wish My Younger Self Knew

By

Christa Rose

Dedication

To my family, friends, and everyone I've met along the way- thank you for teaching me through love and loss, through joy and pain. All of it made me who I am, giving me the strength to inspire and bring hope to others.

To my readers - your support and advice have helped me connect with so many around the world, and I'm truly grateful.

To myself for the bravery it takes to be open and vulnerable.

To my younger self, your quiet strength shaped me; you were deeply and unconditionally loved even when you couldn't feel it, and remember, you are worthy.

DISCLAIMER

Some of the names, descriptions and details may have been
changed to protect the identities of others.

Contents

Introduction

Dear younger me,

As I start this letter, I am filled with so much love and emotion. I wish I could go back in time and give you a big hug because I know right now you feel lost, scared, and confused about what the future holds. You'll discover that pain can lead to growth, and all those tears and heartbreak can pave the way for a life you never imagined—a life where you are more resilient even when you want to give up. You don't need to be flawless. You don't have to change to earn the love of others. You are deserving, just as you are. Don't lose faith in yourself even when you stumble and fall because the truth is, you are capable of achieving anything you set your mind to. You don't have to compare yourself to anyone else, you are perfect the way you are. You need to know you're going to go through some very rough times, and when the darkness feels like it's closing in, I want you to know it's not going to last forever. I know it feels like the emptiness and loneliness are going to swallow you whole. You hold the pen, where you write your own story. I promise there will come a day when you feel seen, heard, and loved. But here's what I want you to remember most. I am so proud of you. You will inspire more people than you know, and you will touch lives in ways that will change them forever. And most of all, remember, you are worthy, you are enough, you are loved unconditionally.

Love,

me

Note: These pages don't just speak to your younger years; they're life advice regardless of age. See for yourself!

TRUTH: 1

Your Mirror, Your Reality

> *"Watch your thoughts, they become your words; watch your words, they become your actions; watch your actions, they become your habits; watch your habits, they become your character; watch your character, it becomes your destiny."*
> – Lao Tzu

Younger Self: What is reality? *Well, I can tell you that sometimes it feels so messed up. No matter how I think about things or what I want to say, there is always someone else doing it better. Half the time, it feels like everyone's faking it, and we're all just pretending to have it together.*

The Shattering Truths I Wish My Younger Self Knew:

Reality isn't something that just happens; it's what is happening. The truth is, how we think, what words we use, and how we choose to act become our reality.

Life is a mirror of what you believe you see. It can be what you see about yourself, whether it be things you like or your flaws. It could be anything and everything around you. You may see things that trigger an old memory, and that becomes your reality.

If you believe you're not good enough, you'll find proof of it everywhere. You will feel every rejection or every mistake. Even every little thing that goes wrong is such a big deal. That will consume your mind, you will start feeling worse about yourself, and maybe you won't even try certain things because why bother? If that's what you believe.

But what if you can shatter that mirror? What if you realize you are capable, that no matter what happens, you deserve good things? When you do this, the world will start showing you proof of that instead.

Have you ever noticed that when you're in a bad mood, everything seems worse? Someone can simply bump into you, and suddenly, you take it as if it's some personal attack. You spill something on a paper, and it feels like the universe is out to get you. But when you're in a good mood, those same things can happen, but you see it differently. Someone can bump into you, you can look back, and maybe you're the one who bumped into them. You leave it like that. You spill something on your paper, and you quickly try to dry it or at least start coming up with solutions.

Your reality is what is happening now and how you are experiencing it. Like a mirror, you can shift the angle, you can change the lighting, you can move it up and down, basically, you can choose a different reflection.

Most importantly, as we create our reality, the truth is a mirror that reflects back what we put out. If the world isn't one you want, it's time to start shattering it and see the truth that we are worthy, beautiful, and loved, and so that is what we will reflect back.

"Your reality is not determined by what happens to you, but by how you think, talk, and act in response to it."
— Unknown

Example

Years ago, I was reading this article about a terrible fire on the top floor of an apartment building. The title was in bold: **"Losing It All: One Disaster, Two Very Different Perspectives"** It was reported that Mary and Kyle watched from a neighbor's house and went on to describe how everything they owned was destroyed. Mary, after realizing the extent of the loss, broke down in tears. "My life is ruined," she said. "All my stuff, the new things I've been saving for—it's all gone! I don't even have a phone; all my contacts, pictures, and everything else were on that phone!"

The reporters learned that Mary had grown up in a household where everything was always taken care of. She had never experienced a loss of this magnitude, and the idea that everything could be stripped away in an instant left her emotionally shaken.

The story switched to Kyle, Mary's neighbor, who was having a bite to eat in the other room. He finally was able to give his family and friends hugs and said, "Thank God we're all ok, even our cat whiskers!" Mary walked in and said, "Isn't this horrible, Kyle? Our entire life is ruined!"

In this heartfelt moment, reporters witnessed Kyle giving Mary a tight hug. "I was so worried about your family when I didn't see you at first, but I'm so happy you all made it out and no one was hurt." "But you lost everything!" Mary cried. "Those are all things that can be replaced, but I'm just glad everyone's ok. Plus, I've been thinking about moving anyway," Kyle said calmly.

Thinking back, I see that this article highlighted the difference between the two reactions. One focuses on the pain of what was lost. The other focused on the relief of what was saved.

Even though they went through the same experiences, their perspectives shaped totally different realities. It's a great example of how loss and hope can exist in completely different realities at the same time.

Think About It:

Have you ever kept putting something off, then finally did it—and the reality turned out much better than you expected?

Ask Yourself

> ➤ What are some ways you could shift your reality from one that holds you back and brings down your mood to one that is optimistic?

TRUTH: 2

WAIT- What Am I Thinking

> *"The moment you shift from living unconsciously to being fully present and aware, everything changes. No longer trapped by old habits or automatic reactions, you begin to see your life with fresh eyes. The power to heal, to grow, and to choose a new path is in your hands. Every thought, every action, becomes a choice—one that reflects who you truly are, not who you were conditioned to be. This shift is where true freedom begins."*
> – Unknown.

Younger Self: *I have so much going on in my life, it feels like my head is going to explode! One minute, I think, "Okay, I can handle this!" Then boom! Something comes rushing back, and I'm back to overthinking everything again!*

The Shattering Truths I Wish My Younger Self Knew:

*I'm going to tell you one simple word that changed my life. **W.A.I.T** What Am I thinking? Have you ever stopped and realized **you are one decision away from changing your life?** That's right, your next decision affects how you feel, what you say, and how you act. That* *is how powerful your thoughts are.*

Here's what you need to ask yourself when that overthinking starts:

- ***Am I stressing over something that hasn't even happened yet?*** *Like, "Oh My God, I'm so stressed out about this exam, I am pulling my hair out! I just know I'm going to fail and ruin my life!" (Well, for me, I still have hair and it didn't ruin my life)*

- ***Am I imagining a worst-case scenario*** *where I'm fired, dumped, and then accidentally run into my ex at a gas station while wearing my worst outfit?*

- ***Is this thought actually true, or am I just telling a story to myself, inserting how I feel instead of what I did,*** *like, "I ate basically a whole pizza in 5 minutes and I swear I now weigh 50 pounds more! I feel so guilty." (Really? Was it the whole pizza in 5 min? And if you did, it must be some world record in speed eating, and no, just for the record, it won't cause an instant 50 pounds.)*

- ***Am I overthinking what someone said?*** *I lent the first few chapters to my friend before the final edit. They said, "Interesting, this reminds me of something else I read. I have to run!" All you keep thinking is, "They hate it." I could tell they said interesting in a sarcastic way. I'm a fraud. Burn it all and start over! (Reality check. Stop creating your own drama! If you obsess over every word, you'll never get past chapter one!)*

- *Is it something that will matter tomorrow, next week, or next year?*
- *Is it making me feel good, or making me feel worse?*
- *Is what I'm thinking even true?*

Now, I'll hit you with some wisdom:

"The happiness of your life depends upon the quality of your thoughts." – Marcus Aurelius

How many times are you having these thoughts? But you're not stuck. Another truth is that you can shift your mindset, and you can change your life! From the moment you wake up to when you hit the pillow at night, you have the power to shape your reality. Your mind believes what you tell it, so fill it with hope and possibilities.

Have you ever felt as if your life was on autopilot? As if you were just going through the actions without even realizing it? The battle between your conscious and subconscious mind shapes your reality every day. Your conscious mind makes you aware of what you're doing, while your subconscious mind can make you oblivious to it.

A few weeks ago, I was driving to the mall and missed my usual exit. Instead, I turned off at an exit where I used to work—more than 15 years ago! Later, when I got home, my husband laughed and asked, "Did you see that giant gorilla that said, 'Happy 50th Birthday, Mildred?'" "No," I said (after threatening his life if he did that to me!) How could I have missed that? It turns out my subconscious mind had taken over, rerouting me to a place I used to go and preventing me from noticing things around me. I mean, who could miss a giant gorilla?

Think of your mind like an iceberg. The small part above the water represents your conscious thoughts—like making that right exit or seeing the gorilla—while the massive part below the surface is your subconscious, where beliefs and past experiences shape your actions without you even realizing it (the part that hijacked your brain to believe you were driving the right way). Now that you are aware, you can now steer your subconscious with intentional choices instead of living on autopilot.

Can you remember one of those nights when you couldn't sleep, but on others, you would wake up feeling pumped and ready to tackle the day, until yesterday's worries came flooding back? Suddenly, you start replaying conversations in your head, overthinking everything, and stressing about stuff that isn't even real. But it started off feeling good, right? That's when it's important to remind yourself, "It's all in my head, and I can choose to either stress over it or let it go; today's a new day, let's turn on some music, and start my day back feeling pumped."

The startling fact is, according to Dr. Joe Dispenza, people think 60,000-70,000 thoughts per day, and 90% of them are the same thoughts as the day before, and those thoughts lead to the same choices, so really nothing changes.

I'm not saying it's easy, but the more you do it, the more the word "W. A. I. T" will pop into your mind. It helps bring you to the present moment, what is actually happening. You can then notice the patterns you create. You will be able to wait and check your thoughts before you respond or react to a situation. Shift your thoughts, and amazing things can happen.

Now, when you are constantly thinking about everything wrong in your life or stuck in old thoughts about the past, you're rehearsing those problems and keeping yourself stuck. It's almost like a nightmare. You wake up with your heart beating, mind racing as if it really happened. It's like your mind saying, "Congratulations, you just experienced a trauma that never happened!"

When you shift your thinking and focus on what you love and the amazing memories you have, you begin to rehearse how it feels to experience great things. And just like that, you start attracting more love into your life. The shattering truth is we've been conditioned by our families and society to focus on our problems. But now that you know the power of WAIT, What Am I Thinking, you can use it to catch your thoughts and flip the script, shifting them toward a life that's filled with peace, love, and joy! "Congratulations! You just experienced something wonderful! Now pass that feeling on!"

"Your mindset is the lens through which you view your world— change it, and your world will change."
– Unknown

Example

"The stories we tell ourselves about ourselves determine our reality."– Brené Brown

You might not believe me, but we make up all kinds of stories in our minds. Let's say you overheard a group of friends saying they may be doing something tonight. So, you clear your schedule, get dressed up, and keep checking your messages. Nothing. OK, well, you reach out to Stacy, she's in the group chat, and ask if they're doing something. "Nope," you quietly hear. "OK, no problem." I was just wondering, "Take care." So, what are you telling yourself?

They didn't invite me.
They don't like me.
Why do I bother? I don't feel like I fit in anyway.

And then you back it up with evidence, thinking she's talking quietly because she doesn't want anybody to hear. You spend the rest of the evening curled up in bed, feeling horrible, maybe even crying, and keep saying, "I hate these people, I'm so stupid for even thinking they would want me around, and you feel like you were back in elementary school because back then sometimes you weren't invited to someone's birthday party, or left out of something so all those thoughts and feelings come rushing back."

Now, I guess that's one possibility, but could there be another one? So now, look at one of the girls, Stacy's perspective. She was in the group when they talked about going out. Stacy really wasn't feeling well, but thought that after taking some medication, she would feel better. Her throat was on fire, she had a hard time breathing, and yes, you guessed it, she had Covid-19. So, she started a new group message, and yes, you were in, and they all decided not to go out.

So, this is why Stacy was talking so quietly. She was sick, and since you said, "Take care," she figured you knew. The reason why you didn't see her message is because you were hurt, so you shut your phone off.

You see how easy it is to ruin your whole day or your whole night obsessing over something that may not have even happened! So what's the point here?

Sometimes, our minds make up entire stories that aren't even close to the truth. We assume, we overthink, and we hurt ourselves based on what we *think* is happening, but not what actually *is*.

Think About It: *Can you think of a time when you might have made up a story in your life about any situation that made you feel worse?*

Ask Yourself
 ➢ How can I use W.A.I.T., What Am I Thinking, to shift my thoughts from worrying about the future, stressing about something you have no control over, or reading too much into what others think, to empowering ones?

TRUTH: 3

WAIT -Why Am I Talking

"Your word is the power that you have to create; it is a gift."
— Don Miguel Ruiz

Younger Self: *My words really don't matter; they are empty noise; honestly, no one is listening anyway. I hate passing a mirror; all I can tell myself is how many things I wish I could change.*

The Shattering Truths I Wish My Younger Self Knew:

Why Am I Talking? *Your Words Are Powerful: You have the power to change your life and someone else's. Choose wisely. What you say can shatter someone else's beliefs or self-esteem, or you can choose words that could heal, uplift, and praise someone else. But your words have just as much, if not more, power about how you talk to yourself.*

What's the first thing people do when they see each other? Usually complain as if it's a competition about who has the shittier life or bond over the latest gossip. But here's the truth: the more you complain, the worse you feel, and the more you gossip, the less you will trust others, and then become more self-conscious. Ask yourself: Am I lifting someone up or tearing them down? Am I spreading kindness or negativity? Would I want these words said about me? You will never know what you say can affect someone else.

"Words can inspire. And words can destroy. Choose yours well."
– Robin Sharma

And when I was talking about myself, out loud or silently, my words were even worse. If I told you to write down everything you told yourself, what do you think it would say? And when it comes to how we talk to ourselves, what does that usually sound like?

- *"I'm a terrible friend because I forgot their birthday."*
- *"I'm not good enough, I can't seem to keep it all together like everyone else."*
- *"I hate the way I look; I can't stand my…"*

I remember that after my car accident, I was beating myself up for not being able to make perfect home-made meals. Sometimes a simple sandwich had to do. I thought I was a terrible mom. Until a friend looked at me and said, "You are going through one of the hardest times of your life! I bet you make sure the sandwich is made exactly how you know they like it." That's when it hit me. I had been talking myself into believing I was a terrible mom, but the reality was that I was doing an amazing job with the circumstances I was in.

Are you appreciating all your amazing qualities, being grateful for what you have, or putting yourself down? Do you shame yourself? Would you talk to your best friend that way? Time to be your own best friend.

We are so programmed to blurt out whatever comes to our minds. Are you trying to impress someone? Listening is as important as talking. Trust me, by waiting before you talk, you show respect, which is much better than regret.

Words Are Powerful- Reframe your words, reframe your life! Instead of saying:

- *"Sorry, I'm late"* **change to** *"Thanks for waiting".*

- *"Tell me"* **change to** *"I'm listening"*.
- *"I can't do it"* **change to** *"I'll give it my best shot"*.
- *"Leave me alone"* **change to** *"I need some space by myself"*.
- *"I feel lazy"* **change to** *"I'm resting"*.
- *"I feel selfish"* **change to** *"I'm practicing self-care."*
- *I hate the way I (insert anything)* **and change it** *to I'm grateful for the ability to ....*

And don't forget about the power of "yet," for example, "I can't do this, yet!"

"I have never regretted my silence. As for my speech, I have regretted it over and over again." – Umar Ibn Al-Khattab R.A.

Often we are so used to blurting out or trying to force our opinions that we forget simply being silent can be the best way to W.A.I.T and ask ourselves, why am I talking and being silent may be the best answer, because as the saying goes, often what we say we regret, and once said we cannot take back.

> **"Wise men speak because they have something to say; fools because they have to say something."** – Plato

Example

A friend of mine from college—let's call him Jordan—had this experience at a local café where they used to hang out with a group of people they knew over time. Jorden looked sad even though he told me he was hanging out with some of his friends when everyone was crowded around a table, eating and complaining about everything. People were venting about money problems, relationship issues, and even making snarky comments about strangers passing by.

Trying to keep up with the group, Jordan blurted out, "I'm terrible at everything lately. I can barely keep up with this online course I'm taking for a job I want." He added with a half-laugh, "Seriously, I'm a mess. Oh, and that new guitar I bought? Total rip-off."

One of the guys started to gossip about this new guy, Tyler, who had recently started coming to the café's open mic nights. Someone said, "That guy's so awkward." Another person added, "Has he even listened to himself? And that crappy guitar?"

Jordan laughed along and said (even though he confided in me he didn't mean it), "Yeah, it's kind of embarrassing."

The group kept joking, but their comments got harsher as time went on.

Afterwards, Jordan told me he felt pretty bad walking away. He realized he'd only said those things to fit in. What made it worse was that Tyler had actually helped him tune his guitar just a week earlier—when nobody else had bothered.

The next time Jordan showed up at the café, the same group was there talking like usual. But Jordan didn't join them. Instead, he went over to Tyler, who was tuning his guitar again, and said, "Hey, thanks for your help a couple of weeks ago. I sounded way better because of you."

Tyler just smiled and said, "No problem. Anytime."

Jordan glanced back toward the group and caught a few stares. For a moment, that old pit in his stomach returned, and he asked himself, "What if they're talking about me now?" But this time, Jordan stood a little taller. It felt better to be real than just to be bitchin' to fit in.

Think About It: *When was there a time you regretted what you said to yourself or someone else?*

Ask Yourself

> ➤ How would you use W.A.I.T? Why Am I Talking to change the way you respond to gossip, complaining, beating yourself up, apologizing all the time to others and yourself to words that are calming and uplifting?

TRUTH: 4

WAIT -What Actions I'm Taking

---

*"Take action! An inch of movement will bring you closer to
your goals than a mile of intention."*
– Dr. Steve Maraboli

Younger Self: *Really, does what I do actually matter in this world?
I mean, I go out of my way and try to be nice, and I barely get a
thank you!*

The Shattering Truths I Wish My Younger Self Knew:

*What Actions I'm Taking? It's crazy to think how even the little
things, the small decisions we don't even think twice about, really
make a difference. Maybe it's getting out of bed early or sleeping in,
choosing to eat something healthy or not. Maybe finally sitting down
to work on something you've been putting off, it all matters.*

*Now, what action I'm taking isn't only about making progress
towards a goal. It's shifting the way we see ourselves in the world
around us. Everything is about reclaiming our power, finding the
courage to show up for other people, and realizing that the best
version of ourselves is the one who acts with kindness, generosity,
and moves forward even when it feels uncomfortable.*

Do you find yourself waiting for the right moment or when you feel like it is time to take action? We come up with all sorts of excuses, maybe tomorrow, or I have other things to do, but are we stalling, or are we making our goals a priority?

There is no perfect time; taking action, no matter how small, creates momentum. What I've learned is that the key to taking action is doing something even when you don't feel like it. When you start feeling overwhelmed, that's when you start to procrastinate more. Try breaking things down into small steps, but most importantly, remember to celebrate each win along the way, no matter how small. When you stop procrastinating and start moving forward, you begin to feel the momentum building, like you've unlocked a new level of energy.

Now, for me, I'm not going to say you'll never feel overwhelmed, but I made it this far, and once I'm done with this page, I will move to the next. If I need to close it, that's OK too. I am celebrating what I've done instead of feeling overwhelmed about how much further I have to go. I will admit I can't wait to get to the conclusion, but I'm going to use that as motivation!

"A journey of a thousand miles begins with a single step."
— *Lao Tzu*

Are you responding with kindness or reacting with anger? Do you cut someone off stealing their parking spot or let them go ahead? When you walk into a store, do you shove the door open or hold it for the person behind you? It could be a simple smile or throwing something in the garbage instead of on the ground. Do you send a message to someone "just because," or is it because you want something in return? Do you laugh and take a picture of a lady who tripped and had a fancy whipped cream-topped coffee end up on her face like a bearded man while others are laughing and some recording a video for a funny post, or do you quickly hand her a napkin? These actions might seem trivial to you, but maybe not to the other person. Each thoughtful action has the power to cause a ripple effect, touching others' lives and inspiring them to do the same. The best way to see someone for who they are is by watching their actions. Actions speak louder than words. Remember this when you are taking any action. The more and more you help out others and teach them what you've learned, it is not only an act of helping someone; it is also providing the other person with ways to keep moving towards their goals or learning new skills.

"Tell me and I forget. Teach me and I remember. Involve me and I learn." –Benjamin Franklin

Most importantly, are you taking action toward self-love, or do you put yourself last? Treat yourself with kindness and love because you are worth it. Ask for what you need because if you try to do it all yourself, it will only lead to burnout.

When you take action from a place of kindness, you will be amazed at how many doors will open, and this will lead to others following your kindness. We can all use a little more act of kindness in this world.

These are a few actions you can take and share with others:

- *Missing someone?*   *...Make a call.*
- *Feeling lonely?*   *...Invite someone over or meet up.*
- *Want to be understood? ...Explain what you mean.*
- *Have questions?*   *...Ask; we don't have to try to figure it out alone.*
- *Love someone?*   *...Tell Them. Don't wait.*
- *Feeling stuck?*   *...Take action. Even a small step creates momentum.*

"Act as if what you do makes a difference. It does."
— William James

Wayne Dyer said it best when he explained that when someone who experiences an act of kindness has their serotonin levels increased, but not only that, the person doing the act even with a simple smile will have an increase of their serotonin levels, and when someone observes this, the same thing happens. So, a simple smile, or any action can make a difference in your life, and others' that you wouldn't even know. Think about this, you can start making a difference, a happier world with just one small act.

So, what action are you taking today? What's one thing, no matter how small, that you can do to make a difference in your life and the lives of those around you? Because the only way to change things, to help others, and create ways for more opportunities, is to start taking action, right now.

It's time to stop waiting. The world is waiting for you to show up.

Example

It was a Thursday night, and I remember this so clearly because a friend of mine, Christina, had just shut down her laptop after finally finishing an assignment. She told me this story not long ago, and it's one of those moments that's just stayed with me.

About six months earlier, she ran into an old friend, *Jade*. Totally randomly, they bumped into each other while grabbing coffee. They had one of those easy, feel-good conversations that reminded them of old times. Jade was talking about maybe moving closer to her boyfriend, and Christina was busy finishing up school and juggling a million things. As they said goodbye, Christina threw out the usual, "Let's catch up next week."

But, like it often happens, life got in the way. Next week turned into six months—just like that.

What's wild is that on the same night, Thursday, Christina had just finished writing a paper about taking action. Not waiting for the perfect timing, not overthinking just taking the step. She said she literally laughed at herself, sat back in her chair, and said, "Okay... this is it. Time to actually do what I keep talking about."

So she took a breath, grabbed her phone, and hit the call button.

"Jade? Hey, it's Christina. It's been a while!"

She said right away she could feel something was off. Jade didn't sound like her usual bubbly self. Christina tried to keep it light and asked, "So, where are you living now? Did you end up making that move?"

There was a pause. Then Jade said quietly, "I'm actually looking for a place. Me and my boyfriend broke up last week, and I don't really have anywhere to go. I moved out here for him, and I don't know many people."

Christina said her heart sank. Without even thinking, she said, "Hey, you don't have to go through this alone. I'm here, okay?"

They ended up talking for a couple of hours. They laughed, got real, and brainstormed some ideas. And near the end of the call, Jade said, "Thank you for calling. This honestly made all the difference. I was feeling really lost, and now I feel like I have some direction again."

Christina promised to call again the following Friday. "Not months from now," she joked. And they both laughed.

After they hung up, Christina told me she just sat there with this lump in her throat, thinking, *What if I had waited even longer?*

And that's what really landed for her and for me when she told me. W.A.I.T. One simple action. Just a phone call led to a bunch of small actions, and Christina realized it wasn't just an assignment she had to do. It was a reminder that what we do or don't do makes a difference. From then on, she acted on her gut, whether it be to call someone, help out someone who is struggling, or when something unexpected pops up instead of letting that opportunity slip away.

Think About It: *Have you ever found yourself in this kind of situation before?*

Ask Yourself

> ➢ How will your life change if you take any action towards what you ultimately want?

TRUTH: 5

Have Gratitude for What You Have Because It Might Be Someone Else's Dream

> *"Gratitude turns what we have into enough and more. It turns denial into acceptance, chaos into order, confusion into clarity...it makes sense of our past, brings peace for today, and creates a vision for tomorrow."*
> - Melody Beattie

Younger me: What are you expecting? I did say thank you! What else should I do? Send flowers? It feels like I'm just a parrot, repeating what I was taught to say to be polite. It's not like my life is a bunch of roses.

The Shattering Truths I Wish My Younger Self Knew: *Gratitude is feeling appreciation for what you have instead of wishing for more, and acts of love, big or small. I know you think it's just a habit to say those words we learned, but I've come to realize it's more profound than that. It's about the feeling and intention behind it. Sometimes, the toughest times in our lives turn into our biggest blessings. That's when I really grasped what gratitude means, often when I least expected it.*

Now, I'm going to share some things you will go through that you can't change, but I promise it has a happy ending. I survived a head-on collision with a pickup truck, held my husband on the stretcher as he took his last breath, and I'm battling a chronic illness. I'm telling you this because if I hadn't been in that car accident, I wouldn't have learned to value time. If my husband hadn't passed away, I wouldn't have discovered what true love is. And if I wasn't dealing with a chronic illness, I wouldn't appreciate my health as much. Even something as annoying as bug splatters on your windshield can spark gratitude when the rain washes them away.

It's hard to see at the time, but these moments remind us to treasure what we have, stop comparing ourselves to others, and find joy in the little things every day. Yesterday a car cut me off when I was driving and instead of reacting (probably with colorful language), I thought, "Thank goodness he didn't hit me!" Then, finished it off with maybe he's rushing because of an emergency, his loved one may be in the hospital. We have no idea what is going on with other people's lives, but we can choose how we react. Because of the feeling of gratitude, I let go of stress and felt overall at peace. Now that you get what gratitude really is, think about what your friends, family, and even strangers have done for you. Focus on what you have, not what you don't. It is easy to lose sight of what we have and take it for granted. Instead of searching for what's missing, take a moment and feel grateful because, in the blink of an eye, it can all be gone.

So, to my younger self, here's the key point: start showing gratitude right away. Don't wait for the big events to come along. Instead, notice the small moments. Value the surprises, the little wonders, and the simple pleasures in your daily life. Being grateful won't just enhance your life; it will help you become a better person, too. And trust me, you'll be really happy you made this choice. What we see as ordinary might actually be someone else's dream.

"Gratitude is not just a feeling. It is a choice you make every day to focus on the good things in your life, even when it's hard. It's a practice that invites more abundance, more joy, and more beauty into your experience."
– Oprah Winfrey

Example

There was this teacher I had in high school who was quiet, a little awkward and always wore the same brown cardigan. I didn't think much of him at the time. He wasn't the cool one or the funny one. But he always noticed when someone was having a hard day. He never made a big deal out of it, just slid a note on your desk with something like, *"You're doing better than you think."*

Back then, I brushed it off. Now I see how rare that kind of quiet kindness is.

I never thanked him. Not once.

But those little notes? I pinned them to my cork board, right next to the concert tickets and other little mementos. But I would glance at these notes, especially on the days when life felt heavy and I didn't believe in myself. That's when his words came back, reminding me someone once saw something in me I couldn't see in myself. I never realized how I could be grateful for a small note. It made me start to think of things that I did for someone, to help them out or just be there.

My mind went blank. I know I've done things, but I now see the value of it, and I'm going to be more intentional, and I don't need to be thanked.

So, wherever he is, I hope he knows. Sometimes, the people who change us the most are the ones we forget to thank.

Think About It: *Has there been a time when you had a realization like this before?*

Ask Yourself

- ➢ Where are areas of your life where you can be more grateful for instead of taking things for granted?

TRUTH: 6

Do You Want Peace Or Be Right?

> *Remember that it is far more fulfilling to embrace the ability to find peace rather than sprinting to claim the trophy of being right. Some relationships can be destroyed from this simple lesson.*

Younger Self: *But I'll look dumb if I can't prove I'm right! Let's not fool ourselves. If I give up, they win, and others look at me as the loser. If they just stop talking and listen to what I am actually saying, they would see my point and find out I was right all along, and they are wrong!*

The Shattering Truths I Wish My Younger Self Knew:

Winning an argument isn't the same as winning in life. I know how frustrating it is when someone's trying to argue with you, but you know you're right! I used to think, "If only they could see it through my eyes, they would agree with me!" It felt as if it turned into a game of who's going to win the argument instead of what the actual issue was! To be transparent, they would be talking, and I wouldn't even be listening. I'd already be forming my next defense. Instead, put yourself in their shoes. Sometimes, stop talking and actually listen to what the other person is saying. They may not be right, but they might have valid points. When you do this, you show the other person respect and make it a conversation, not a competition. You don't always have to have the last word.

You don't need to prove yourself of anything. If you're trying to convince the other person that you're right, then question why you do. Are you insecure? Do you need validation? Being right doesn't make you more worthy or valuable. Self-worth comes from who you are, not from winning arguments.

"It's not about being right. It's about doing what's right."
– Unknown

Sometimes, it's better to just agree to disagree instead of dragging things out. Value your relationships. Life is too short and too valuable to let an argument over who's right change or possibly end a relationship. This can happen with lifelong friends, co-workers, and family. At the end of the day, if the other person won't let it go and move on, then question if you want them in your life or how much. This is a perfect time to set boundaries and make it clear that the topic that turned into a black hole will not be brought up. Hold that boundary. From then on, if things started to go down that road, it didn't matter if they said $1+1 = 5$, I would laugh and say, I guess if you say so, smile, and go on with the day. Because I definitely felt happier and left with integrity and humility. Because at the end of the day, don't let anyone steal your peace!

"Let go of the need to be right. Choose peace instead."
– Eckhart Tolle

Example

Colleen and Jacky have been best friends for years. It was Friday night, and Colleen was excited to wear her favorite jacket. When Colleen slipped it on, she noticed a big stain. She let Jacky borrow it, but when she got it back, Jacky didn't say a thing about the stain. Jacky showed up to get ready to go out, and Colleen blurted out, "Seriously, you gave me back my jacket without telling me about the stain?" Jacky looked away and said, "It's just a jacket. You have a bunch." Colleen was desperately trying to spray some soap on it and wouldn't even look at Jacky.

Jacky said, "It's just a jacket. Why are you so upset?"

That only made Colleen more frustrated. "Because it's mine, and I pay for my own clothes—not like you. And you know this was my favorite!"

Jacky just shrugged and said, "You're making such a big deal about this. Calm down."

"You never take care of my stuff!" Colleen snapped. "I don't even know what I was thinking when I let you wear it."

"I'm not like that," Jacky shot back. "You're overreacting."

And in a split second, it wasn't about the jacket, it was about respect, and feeling they weren't heard. By the time they stopped, they didn't know what to say. They both felt hurt.

Think About It: *Can you think of a time when you went through something similar?*

Ask Yourself

➢ How do you handle a situation when you're both upset, you know you are right, but find a way to move past it and find common ground?

TRUTH: 7

Destiny By Design

> *When you think of it, really, there are four fundamental questions of life. You've asked them, I've asked them, every thinking person asks them. They boil down to this: origin, meaning, morality, and destiny. 'How did I come into being? What brings life meaning? How do I know right from wrong? Where am I headed after I die?'* – Ravi Zacharias

Younger Self: *I just can't catch a break. Like, do some people just get lucky and have great lives while others don't? I don't get it. If I work hard, does that even matter? Or is everything already decided for me?*

The Shattering Truths I Wish My Younger Self Knew:

Now, your destiny is what you choose to create next. Reality isn't permanent, it is only what is happening to you right now. Designing your destiny isn't about having good luck or bad luck, but it is what you do with what happens. Your life might not be meant to follow the path you thought was perfect. "Bad luck" might be the best thing that ever happened because it allows a space for opportunities to grow. But here's the truth: Reality is just what's happening right now. Destiny is what you choose to create next.

Your Future Is Built One Choice at a Time

No one handed successful people a blueprint for life. They created their own. Every thought, every decision, every action is shaping your future (even if it means sunscreen or an embarrassing burn), whether you realize it or not. For years, I was stuck in reaction mode—just dealing with whatever life threw at me. But the second I took ownership of my choices, things changed. I stopped reacting and started creating. And so can you.

Three Shifts to Start Designing Your Destiny

1. ***Own Your Story***

   Take responsibility for where you are. Stop blaming others or outside circumstances. This is when you take your power back. You've lived through the past and now have the ability to make some shifts to become the best version of yourself.

2. ***See Possibility, Not Just Reality***
   Do I like my life, or do I love my life? Your current situation is not your final destination. The key to growth is making choices based on where you want to be, not just where you are. Ask yourself: What would the future me want me to do right now?

3. ***Act As If***

   Want to change your life? Start acting like the person who already has the life you want. Think like them. Speak like them. Make decisions like them. Not in a fake way, but in a way that aligns your actions with your future vision. You don't wait to be successful and then start acting successful. You act successful first, and then you become it.

Wealth isn't built overnight but by repeated smart choices. Freedom isn't handed to you; it's claimed through daily courage. World-changing impact doesn't happen in one moment but through relentless dedication.

To put it simply, your life is shaped by what you think. Feed your mind with garbage, and that's how you feel. I remember listening to a podcast and they mention something like this. Emotions aren't bad, they are alarms to your thoughts, so pay attention. Fear means that you think something that matters to you may not work out. Anger shows you think your boundary was crossed. And anxiety? You're thinking too much about the future instead of being here in the now. It's not motivation that ruins your life, it's a habit you think is normal. Change how you think about your habit and change everything. Your past? Think of it like a book. Read it, learn from it, then close the book. If someone triggers you, it usually means you're stuck in what your mind is telling you about yourself, and that needs to be healed or accepted. In control? It's a total myth. You can't control everything, but you can control your thoughts and your next move. In the end, the way you think shapes the life you live.

Destiny creates your legacy. What kind of legacy do you want to create?

"You are not the victim of the world, but rather the master of your own destiny. It is your choices and decisions that determine your destiny." – Roy T. Bennett

Example

So, this is when I get vulnerable. You know, for a long time, I really believed I had no say in how my life was going. It felt like everything just kept happening to me. I lost people I loved, people I thought would always be around. I went through some really scary accidents. And then on top of all that, I was trying to live with this rare disease that no one really understood. I felt like I was just... stuck, honestly.

It wasn't like I didn't want more. I just didn't know how to take back control because, at that point, it didn't feel like I had any.

Then one day, I didn't even remember what I was doing, I think I was just scrolling and needed something to listen to when I came across this podcast. I think it was called *Life by Design* or something along those lines. I hit play without thinking much of it. But then the host said something that made me stop everything: **"Reality is what's happening right now. But destiny? That's what you decide to create next."**

And I just sat there.

Because that one line hit differently. I started thinking: What if I'd been carrying this story for so long that life was just chaos, that I had no control and what if that story wasn't even true?

That one podcast didn't fix everything, but it cracked something open. I started thinking differently, like…what can I do moving forward from the experiences I've been through? Maybe I could help someone else, or at least have more compassion. How do I create a future that I really want instead of staying stuck in the past?

Little things started shifting. I stopped waiting for life to settle down before I made a move. I began acting like someone who was building something, not just surviving something. It wasn't about pretending everything was fine. It was about showing up differently because I believed something better was possible.

And I guess that's what I'd tell anyone who feels stuck the way I used to: You don't have to wait for perfect conditions. Getting out of my comfort zone was the best thing I did. I didn't have to have it all figured out. I see kids spinning on this all the time. Basically, my message would be somewhere in all the chaos, we still have the power to design our destiny.

Think About It: *Did you ever question if your life could be different?*

Ask Yourself

> ➤ What would be the first thing you would do if you could imagine designing your destiny?

TRUTH: 8

The Two Faces of Hope: Pressure and Pain

> "Once you choose hope, anything is possible." —
> Christopher Reeve

Younger Self: *Deep down, I think people only value me for what I do for them, not for who I really am. I mean, what would they think if I said no? But sometimes, my own heart is broken, but I would rather smile and pretend I'm fine. I don't want to burden them, so I will hold in the pain. But to tell you the truth, it feels like the pain will never end.*

The Shattering Truths I Wish My Younger Self Knew:

*H.O.P.E. should've been my mantra because it means **Heck Over Pleasing Everyone**. I really wish my younger self had realized that always putting others first would just leave you feeling exhausted and drained. I know it's easy to feel like other people's happiness is more important than yours, but when was the last time you felt happy?*

*I felt that if I did more, people would need me, like me, and I would be part of everything. Everything changed when I started valuing myself for **who** I am, not just for **what** I do. My worth isn't based on* *how much I give or how many people I please. Once I embraced H.O.P.E., I got my strength back. Saying no is not a weakness; it's a declaration that you are worthy too, and your needs matter. I learned to set boundaries, protect my energy, and take care of myself like I always did for others. Now, I feel lighter, stronger, and more energized.*

And when life gets tough, when the pain feels like it's too much, hold onto another kind of H.O.P.E.: Hold On, Pain Ends. You no longer have to hold onto people just because they need you, but because they want you and value you in their lives. You no longer stay in bed, worrying about falling into some depression. I know the pain will end. All you have to do is reach out, and you will find out it doesn't matter who; it matters that you do. I stick by this saying: "I would rather be remembered for overcoming my tragedies than being a victim of them."

"You can't please everyone, and you can't make everyone like you." *– Katie Couric*

"The pain you feel today is the strength you feel tomorrow. For every challenge encountered, there is opportunity for growth."
— *Unknown*

Example

I felt so bad for my friend who always said yes to anything. Well I called her and she was just recovering from being sick. I asked her what happened and she continued to tell me her story.

"Tammy will have the Christmas party next Friday. Everyone, be there; it will be a blast!" Her co-workers said with excitement. Tammy was just recovering from the flu but didn't want to say no because she didn't want to upset them. All week she spent planning the party, decorating, snacks, and music; she did it all. The night finally came, and she was running around, making sure everything was perfect. Her friends were laughing, dancing, and having fun, but

Tammy felt completely drained and nauseous, but she kept smiling anyway.

She went outside, only to have her phone buzz. It was a text saying they need more of those appetizers. As she walked in, she felt herself becoming lightheaded.

Her friend Amy came up, drink in hand. "Tammy, you're doing everything! You're like the host, DJ, and snack queen. You're crushing it! Oh, and get more pop before you come downstairs." As Amy went down empty-handed, Tammy grabbed the pop, feeling even worse.

Tammy's body couldn't take it anymore, and she started to get sick. Finally, she became angry that everyone used her to do everything. She heard this acronym for HOPE, Heck Over Pleasing Everyone. "I could use some hope right now," she thought. Then she got so sick she started passing out.

Someone popped in, whom she barely knows, said, "Hey, they need you to change the playlist." That was it. She went downstairs, shut off the music, and said, "Party's over. I've been sick this whole time, and I'm done." She felt empowered.

She was surprised that as people left, a few said, "I hope you feel better, and a great party, thank you!" At that moment, she realized she didn't have to say yes to the party when she wanted to say no. It didn't mean people wouldn't like her, and if they didn't, she didn't care.

She soaked in a bubble bath and remembered the other acronym, Hold On Pain Ends. As she crawled into bed, she started to feel better and was proud of herself.

Before I hung up the phone, I told her how proud of her I was too!

Think About It: *Does any part of this feel like your own story?*

Ask Yourself

> ➤ What are some ways you are going to say "no" when you're pressured to say yes, and are there areas of your life where you are stuck with a feeling of pain but afraid to burden anyone?

TRUTH: 9

Secrets: The Silent Chains

> *"Some secrets are meant to be whispered to the wind, not carried to the grave."* – Unknown

Younger Self: *If anyone found out, they would kill me! It doesn't matter because everyone will think it's my fault anyway. It's better to keep my mouth shut. I know the little stuff, who cares, but those things that I feel so guilty about, so afraid to tell anyone, it's better to keep quiet and go on living pretending everything is fine!*

The Shattering Truths I Wish My Younger Self Knew:

Secrets can be anything that you don't want anyone to know. That's something you want to keep private. But the truth is, there are different kinds of secrets, some that are fun (like planning a surprise party with a giant blow-up gorilla in the front yard), some that hold you back from trying something new. Types of secrets range from how we feel, experience, or sometimes to spare someone else's feelings (Like telling them you don't like their outfit) or even their opinion, but it's not worth hurting the relationship.

But there is a dark side to secrets. Some are dangerous, even trauma-related. When you hold them in, it can fester inside you, creating pain, even physical pain, and will haunt you for the rest of your life. It can change the way we respond or react to others or situations. It can hurt relationships, cause isolation, or even substance abuse to numb the pain. How do I know? I've been there. Now, I'm talking about those big secrets, like abuse, theft, or if anyone, anyway, hurt you or someone else, and if they say don't tell anyone, telling someone doesn't mean you're a liar, it means you might be a hero. I know you're scared, but tell a trusted person, or another adult, or even call a hotline. This is the most crucial thing I have to bring awareness to.

"Secrets are like honey in a paper jar. Eventually, they leak out."
— Drew Barrymore

I'm wondering how many people stretch the truth on their resume, change some of the details of a story, or make a mistake but hide it. I'm not here to judge, but I will tell you, being honest is much easier than trying to remember the facts you have changed! (Like, were you really studying or working late? Or were you somewhere else?) Here's the truth. Secrets can be protection, but they can also be a prison. If a secret is keeping you safe, helping you grow, or making life better for someone else, then it's serving a purpose.

Secrets whisper in your ear, "If people find out, they will judge you," and leave you wrapped in guilt and shame. And trauma-related secrets? They're like living in a prison of your own making. Secrets have way less power than we give them. Unlock the prison that's keeping you and your secrets in, and then you have the power because you have the key!

"Secrets are like shadows—they may seem to linger and hide in the corners of the mind, but no matter how carefully we shelter them, they always have a way of creeping into the light. For as much as we try to lock them away, they hold power over us, shaping our thoughts, our actions, and even our relationships. The truth, like the dawn breaking the night, eventually finds its

way out, and when it does, it brings clarity, freedom, and a new beginning. " – Unknown

Example:

Barb was the one everyone leaned on. The cheerful one. The dependable friend who always showed up with a smile and a solution. To the outside world, she seemed like she had it all together.

But no one knew how much she was hiding.

She had been quietly struggling for years. The depression crept in slowly, then settled deep. Some mornings, even sitting up felt impossible. Her phone buzzed with messages she couldn't answer. Her inbox stayed full. She told herself she'd get to it tomorrow, but tomorrow kept slipping away.

And still, she smiled. Pretending was easier than trying to explain something she had been trying to cover up for years.

Ava, her best friend, started to notice the excuses, canceled plans, and missed calls. Barb kept backing out, even from things she used to love. It all felt... off.

One Thursday night, Ava stopped guessing. She just showed up with a pint of ice cream and said, "I miss you. Can I come in?"

They sat in silence on Barb's bed until she finally said, "I think I've been depressed. I didn't want anyone to know. I've been hiding it."

Ava nodded. "My mom hid hers for years, too. When she finally got help, things started to shift. She still has hard days. But now she doesn't face them alone."

Barb didn't speak right away. But something inside her softened. Ava didn't judge her or think any less of her.

"I found a therapist who does video sessions," Ava added. "I can help you reach out. Or just sit with you. I'm not going anywhere."

Barb realized then, letting someone in didn't make her weak. It made her real. And maybe, she could finally stop judging herself for having depression, and this secret she was carrying was only part of her pain, and she realized it was time to end it. She stopped pretending everything was ok, took Ava's advice, and connected with an amazing therapist. Best of all, she didn't have to carry any secrets anymore. For the first time in years, she finally felt safe.

Think About It: *Have you ever felt like you had to keep it all together even when everything inside felt like it was falling apart?*

Ask Yourself

> ➤ What could you do if you felt a heavy burden, guilt, or shame, but keeping a secret felt easier than opening up?

TRUTH: 10

Forgiveness Is Letting Go Of The Pain

> *"I stopped giving up hope that the past could ever be different."* – Oprah Winfrey

Younger Self: *I get that I should forgive, but right now, I'm just not feeling it! It just feels like letting them off the hook for what they did. And I hate that. Does it mean I'm supposed to forget what happened? Pretend like it didn't hurt? And they don't deserve a free pass.*

The Shattering Truths I Wish My Younger Self Knew:

Forgiveness is not about letting go of the past; it's about freeing yourself from the pain it holds over you. Forgiving doesn't mean they didn't hurt you; it just means their actions won't define you anymore. There's no deadline for forgiveness. And it definitely does not say that what they did was okay.

No matter how deep the wound is, holding onto it only keeps it open, making you relive the pain over and over. My ah-ha moment was when I realized it didn't excuse what others have done or make it okay. It's forgiving that it was THEIR:

- *beliefs*
- *choices*

- *Actions*

Not mine. It's cutting the chain to the past and allowing me to move forward. Trust me, they're still left with their chain, but that's no longer attached to you. This is the key to having inner peace.

It's about freedom, not forgetting. You're not going to waste another moment on reliving the pain, instead, you're going to forgive the fact that you've held onto it, let it hold you back, and you will be choosing peace over their power. There's a saying that holding onto resentment is like drinking poison and hoping the other person will die. All you're doing is killing yourself inside. It's easy to stay stuck as the victim. I want to validate that you were the victim. To whoever needs to hear this: I am so sorry. I'm sorry they hurt you. I'm sorry they made you feel small. I'm sorry they took your joy. But now it's time for you to stop suffering. You deserve that.

"I've learned that forgiveness is not just about letting go of anger or resentment, but about freeing yourself from the chains of the past. People will forget what you said, people will forget what you did, but they will never forget how you made them feel — and you will never forget the weight of holding onto a grudge. Forgiveness isn't just for the other person; it's for you. It's about setting yourself free, reclaiming your peace, and choosing love over pain. I've learned that when you forgive, you're not excusing the hurt, but you're choosing to let go of its power over your life." – Maya Angelou

Example

We were sitting around in a small group, just talking, nothing too deep at first. Then someone, who hadn't said much all night, started to share something that's stuck with me ever since.

They said, "When I bought my first car, it should've been a happy moment. I had saved up for it, worked hard. But instead of feeling proud, I just felt... heavy. I kept thinking about my dad. He loved cars. And I kept wishing I could show it to him."

Then they got quiet for a second, and you could tell this wasn't easy for them to talk about.

"That night, I drove to the old house I grew up in. I hadn't been there in years—not since my dad left when I was 13. I remember sitting outside, gripping the steering wheel, hands shaking. Everything just kind of hit me all at once."

They talked about how they had carried that moment for years, like some kind of weight on their chest. Every birthday he missed, every school event, every big life moment—they said it all just got packed away, buried deep.

"I used to pretend it didn't bother me. Said I was fine. But I wasn't. I was angry. Not just at him—but at myself too, for letting him not being there mess with how I saw myself."

Then they said something changed that night. Not because they planned it. Just being back in front of that house brought something up.

"I wasn't there to see him or to forgive him, not really. I didn't even know if he still lived there. I just needed to say it to myself more than anyone else: You were wrong to leave. I didn't deserve that. But I'm not going to carry this anymore. It's not mine to carry.'"

They talked about how forgiveness isn't always some big moment with a hug or a phone call. Sometimes it's just letting go. Not to make it okay, but to stop letting it take up space inside you.

"I cried in that car for probably an hour," they said. "Said everything I'd been holding in. And when I drove off, I felt lighter. Like I'd left some of that pain behind. The resentment, the idea that I wasn't good enough... it stayed there."

They knew their dad might never say sorry. Might never realize what he did. But that night, they said they finally understood that forgiveness isn't for them. It's for you. And they were ready to accept it.

As they drove away, they said something I'll never forget: "I realized I didn't need his approval. I was proud of what I'd done buying that car, getting that far, and for once, that pride felt like it belonged to me. That was enough."

That stuck with me, and my gut was telling me it was time to forgive some people too.

Think About It: *Have you ever struggled to forgive someone who hurt you, even when they said they were sorry?*

Ask Yourself

> ➢ Where were times in your life when someone betrayed your trust, and how can you feel the freedom of forgiveness? Have you ever betrayed someone else's trust? What are ways you can make things right if possible?

TRUTH: 11

Holistic Health: From Woo-Woo to Wellness

> *"Our body and mind have the capacity to heal themselves if we allow them to rest. Stopping, calming, and resting are preconditions for healing."* – Thich Nhat Hanh

Younger Self: *Sure, cover me with incense, I'll lie on a yoga mat while chanting some noise…Great, I feel much better! Now give me a pill and I'll be on my way! Yeah, I heard of "holistic healing," or some people call it energy work. What energy? I mean, we are all made from energy, so what does it do? Does it give us more? I can get my meds that I've been taking for years, so why change what's not broken?*

The Shattering Truths I Wish My Younger Self Knew:

For years, I thought it was woo-woo stuff until after my car accident, dealing with grief and chronic pain. I was popping so many pills; I was taking pills to handle the side effects of the other ones! I was desperate until a friend introduced me to all the different modalities. I started with Reiki, and this was the first time I felt some pain relief, not just physically, but emotionally had blocks. Reiki started to reduce any blockage and bring my body back into alignment. I went from a skeptic to a Reiki Master! Basically, at its core, holistic healthcare is about treating the whole person, not just looking at their symptoms in isolation like popping a pill to get rid of a headache. Definitely, modern medicine is fantastic at diagnosing and treating specific conditions, but it doesn't always look at a person as a whole. There are a lot of times when conventional medicine and holistic medicine can go hand in hand. A lot of people dismiss holistic methods like acupuncture or herbal remedies as woo-woo because they don't think it's backed up by the same scientific research as conventional treatments, but the reality is many holistic practices are grounded in science, and there are so many! Acupuncture has been shown to help with pain management, and certain herbs, like turmeric and ginger, have real, proven anti-inflammatory properties. It's not magic, it's just nature working with science.

There are so many different modalities and options! Just a few are:

- Breath Work
- Sound Vibrations
- Essential Oils
- Light therapy
- Hypnotherapy
- Enjoying a tea leaf reading or Akashic Record (even for entertainment purposes, you might stumble on something)
- Reiki
- EFT (Emotional Freedom Technique)
- There are many mixed modalities, and I can't even begin to list them all.

"True holistic healing is about stepping outside the box—where the mind, body, and spirit converge to unlock innovative paths to wellness."

Example:

So, Allen's been dealing with these relentless headaches that just won't quit. He's tried everything, like stronger pain meds, doctor visits, but nothing's working. The tests all come back normal, and he's left thinking, "Great, so it's all in my head?"

One day, he met up with a friend at his place, and his friend's sister was there, calmly doing her homework like she was in a Zen commercial. Allen, feeling like his brain's about to explode, says, "I wish I could be that focused." She replies, "I just got back from a Reiki session; it really helped."

"Sure, some Reiki practitioner will wave their hands over me and magically fix everything?" he jokes. But after another sleepless night, he figures, *What do I have to lose?*

He made an appointment, and when he got there, he lay on the massage table. He really didn't expect to feel anything, but it was a chance to lie down! But as the practitioner moved her hands above him, a strange warmth spread through his chest. A deep sense of calm washed over him. It's not like falling asleep, it's like his body is finally letting go of something it's been holding onto for too long.

Later that night, he grabbed his computer to do some work, and his headache was gone! Maybe it was the Reiki, or letting go of stress, he didn't know but didn't care, but it worked!

Think About It: Have you ever tried something new, even something you didn't believe in at first, and been surprised by how much it helped?

Ask Yourself

➤ Would you be open to holistic health care, and if not, what's holding you back?

TRUTH: 12

Perfectionism and Fear: The Silent Partners

> *"Perfectionism is the enemy of creativity."* — Unknown

Younger Self: *You want to know what being perfect is? Let me put it this way: Perfectionism is when you get super stressed, and everyone judges you. I know because I feel like if I make one mistake, I definitely would have failed.*

The Shattering Truths I Wish My Younger Self Knew:

Perfectionism isn't about having high standards; it's rooted in fear. Fear of failing. Fear of being judged. Fear of not measuring up. The truth about trying to be perfect is a myth! It tricks you into thinking that making a mistake means you are a failure. We try to fool ourselves and everyone else into thinking that we have everything under control, but the truth is, it's impossible to have control of everything.

I used to believe that if I could just achieve perfection, everything would work out perfectly. People would adore me, I'd be successful, and life would be easy. But instead, I wore myself out trying to meet these impossible expectations, constantly beating myself up when I fell short, and wasting years chasing something that wasn't real. That's not just tiring; it leads to self-doubt and burnout. No matter what you accomplish, perfectionism will always tell you, "It's not good enough."

- Complete a project? You could've done better.
- Make a mistake? It's a sign of failure.
- Show vulnerability? People will judge you.
- Take a break? Others think- must be nice to have all that free time.
- Spent the day cleaning? There are dirty areas.

It keeps moving the finish line every time you get close. If you let it control your life, you'll never feel like you've truly succeeded. I once thought mistakes were my enemies. Now, I realize they're my teachers. Every failure, every "I can't believe I did that" moment has made me wiser, stronger, and more resilient. When you're not running on empty, people can relate to you, and that's when you can relax, aim for progress, and enjoy being your awesome, imperfect self!

"Perfection is the enemy of progress." – Winston Churchill

Example:

I've decided to sign up for a fun night of paint class. I got my canvas all set up for a big art project, it's clean, crisp, and kind of intimidating. I splurged on a fancy tube of electric-blue paint because I *had* to get that sky just right. I held the brush, stared at the blank space, and thought, *If I mess this up, I might as well toss the whole thing.* So… I froze. Brush hovering, canvas glaring back and I was in a moment of total paralysis.

I stood there for so long that my stomach reminded me it was snack time. I reached into my bag, grabbed a granola bar, and two bites in, my elbow knocked the brush, flicking a blob of paint onto the corner of the canvas. I froze. I stepped back and was actually stunned. That little spill (not the huge blob my mind made up) looked like the first cloud of an epic sunset! It pulled the whole piece together and when I squinted it gave it depth, and I looked at the clock and realized I had just wasted time stalling because I put this pressure on myself that it had to be some perfect masterpiece. I saw other people laughing and remembered this was supposed to be a fun night, not a contest.

Inspired, I dove right in, adding soft shifts in color and tone around that "cloud," and before I knew it, I'd created something that genuinely surprised me! Looking around at others and then looking at mine, it felt vivid, expressive, and complete. Yes, it was completely different but unique. And it all started with one splash that broke the spell.

Think About It: Has something ever gone totally wrong—only to turn out even better than you planned?

Ask Yourself

➢ What is the first thing you would do if perfectionism weren't holding you back? (For me, it was writing a book!)

TRUTH: 13

You're Stronger Than What Scares You

> *"The only thing we have to fear is fear itself—nameless, unreasoning, unjustified terror which paralyzes efforts to convert retreat into advance."* – Franklin D. Roosevelt

Younger Self: *What do you mean, I'm afraid, I just don't want to do it. That's my escape line when I am so scared to try something because so many things can happen. What if I get hurt, what if I embarrass myself, what if I fail, OMG I can think of so many things, I know I'm going to fail so why try?*

The Shattering Truths I Wish My Younger Self Knew:

Fear is real, sometimes, it's our best friend, and other times, it's our worst nightmare. It can keep us safe from a threat or danger, but for a lot of people, fear stops them from living, taking risks, making judgments, and forming relationships. What about fear of success? It might sound crazy, but deep down, you know that the more successful you are, it might mean more work and less time with family and friends. So often we self-sabotage ourselves. Now that you are aware of this, you can look at other options that aren't so overwhelming.

*There are so many acronyms for **F.E.A.R.;** False Evidence Appearing Real. Fear hands you false evidence and makes it feel* *like the truth, like tricking you into believing your shadow is a monster. I wouldn't even try something if there were a chance I would fail. I put so much pressure on myself that I would be a ball of stress! We constantly ask ourselves, What will they think of me? How will they see me? Will I look like a fool? There is no way I'm going in the pool with this body, and so much more. The truth is, it can steal the joy and growth and leave you in a cycle of doubt.*

A few points about fear:

- *Fear is a flag, not a stop sign: Fear often signals a place of growth, not danger. Take a gentle step forward to see what might be waiting on the other side. Open the door, it might just hold your next breakthrough—and maybe even a pleasant surprise or two. (could be a career move, or finding your future husband sitting next to you on the plane that you were too scared to fly!)*
- *Gut instinct vs. fear: Learn to differentiate between gut instinct and fear. Your gut is quiet and sure, guiding you to safety. Fear, however, is loud and often misleading, keeping you from stepping into your full potential.*
- *Comfort zones are cages in disguise: While comfort zones feel safe, they also keep you stuck. Growth, excitement, and the life you truly want to happen outside those walls.*

*It can also stand for **Face Everything And Rise**, meaning fear is just an obstacle, but you have the choice to Face Everything and Rise above it. When you let fear rob you of the moments, dreams, and love that could make your life extraordinary, the regret of holding back will stay with you far longer than the sting of any failure. Keep track of all your past successes and praise yourself because it is in these moments that you will be able to find the moments where fear didn't hold you back. Letting fear control you will be something in the end, you will look back and regret it because it is the chance you didn't take, the love you didn't experience, the fun you didn't have, and the dreams you left behind that will hurt the most.*

"I learned that courage was not the absence of fear, but the triumph over it. The brave man is not he who does not feel afraid, but he who conquers that fear. The greatest glory in living lies not in never falling, but in rising every time we fall. Difficulties break some men but make others. No axe is sharp enough to cut the soul of a sinner who keeps on trying, one armed with the hope that he will rise even in the end."

— Nelson Mandela

Example

I am sure by now you realize that I was terrified of failure. *Terrified.* The thought of not being good enough, of falling short, paralyzed me. I remember one of my first big public speaking opportunities, one that I was so excited about because I really wanted to get my message out and tell my story. I had spent weeks preparing, who am I kidding, months before.

Then came the moment of truth: Will I be able to pull this off? My mind kept telling me, "What if they don't like me? What if I mess up?" I mean, I could look like an idiot in front of people! Then I remembered that when you are afraid of something, your hands get sweaty, your breath gets shallow, and you can start to tremble. Well, it is the same symptoms as being excited! So, you can trick your brain into saying, "I'm excited to do this!"

Sure, I might make a mistake, and I might feel embarrassed for a second, but I realized in that moment that failure wasn't the end of the world. It's not like I was actually going to die from making a mistake! (That's what was running through my head: I will die if I mess up!) I realized that the best part was that I took a second and realized the other speakers were just as nervous as I was, and they have been doing this for years!

Oh, and are you wondering how my speech went? It was amazing! I mean, it's amazingly real. I lost track of my timeline, which only made the speech funnier. I stumbled over the microphone stand and chalked it up to a metaphor for stumbling through life. In the end, I got my message out, and that was my objective. The rest? Well, that was some unplanned added bonus.

Think About It: *Have you ever been so afraid to fail that you almost didn't try—only to find out it wasn't as scary as you thought?*

Ask Yourself

> ➤ What are some of the things you would do if you let go of the fear of judgment, failing, embarrassing yourself, or anything else that is holding you back?

TRUTH: 14

Spirituality for Skeptics: It's Not as Weird as You Think

Younger Self: *"I don't get what people mean by 'spirituality.' Like, what's the point of believing in something you can't even see or prove? Don't you have to believe in a set sort of rules, or be part of a particular religion? I know people who have to meditate for hours on end, and I guess they are spiritual, but I just don't have the time. It all sounds weird to me.*

The Shattering Truths I Wish My Younger Self Knew:

Let me be clear. Spirituality does not require a belief in a religion, a particular God, a universe, a source, a higher power, or the many names used. Spirituality is less about what you believe in and more about how you experience the world, how you connect with it.

For some, spirituality can exist within religion and a belief system, and many people find profound spiritual experiences through prayers and rituals. But it can also exist outside of religion.

For me, it's finding peace amongst the chaos, letting go of control, and knowing all will work out for my highest good.

Why does any of this matter? Because at its core, spirituality is about meaning. It's about feeling like life isn't just a series of random events but something deeper, something that will shine a light even when we feel lost. We chase after distractions, material possessions, and external validations, hoping they'll fill the void, but true fulfillment doesn't come from the outside; it comes from within.

There are so many ways you can feel a spiritual connection. It could be:

- *simply touching the edge of the ocean and feeling part of something greater than yourself.*
- *holding a newborn baby and experiencing the miracle of life.*
- *meditation.*
- *creative expression, like connection through music, dance, and more. Missing out on something you believed was essential, like a job, a relationship, or a plan, only to watch something even better come into your life later, making you realize that life was guiding you toward what you truly needed, even when you couldn't see it at the time.*
- *acts of kindness, love.*
- *hugging a tree (if you feel called to) or simply being in nature and really focusing on the beauty.*
- *simply sitting quietly, asking a question, and listening for an answer.*
- *Being grateful when something comes into your life at the perfect time when you need it the most.*

Anyway, that can bring you a sense of peace that you've never experienced before but yearned for.

I found that most of us focus on our relationships, our work, finances, and recreational activities; the list is endless, but we still feel an emptiness. This is often because they are neglecting a part of themselves that is within, which brings a deeper sense of meaning while on this earth.

Think about the many times someone has entered your life at the exact moment you needed them. Maybe they drove by and helped you with a flat tire. For me, it was hundreds of times I can think of now, but one particular time was when I was driving home and started having a seizure. We pulled off, and my husband was giving me medication while trying to keep our kids distracted. I noticed this lady staring at me, and as I was self-conscious, I went to the bathroom to try to splash water on my face. She followed me in and told me she was a retired nurse, and noticed the second I walked in, I was struggling. As I went back to the table, she helped me through it, was able to distract the kids, and then offered us to stay at her house as it was only 20 minutes away, and the weather was bad. That way, she can keep an eye on me, in case I need to get to a hospital. I mean, what is the chance that a complete stranger is in the exact place that I would need, and actually offers us to stay at her house? She confided she wasn't even going to pull over, but at the very last second, something told her to stop and grab something to eat, even though she was in a rush to get home. She told me it was as if something else was taking over the wheel, and she found herself pulling in and grabbing something to eat before she noticed us. Without getting into the rest of the story, I call her my earth angel at the rest stop.

I know I've gone through many tragedies that could have broken me, but instead, they shaped my destiny, and others called me an Earth Angel, but it's just something that resonates with me. I'm naturally drawn to people in need, especially without knowing it, similar to the lady at the rest stop.

Spirituality is an individual relationship, and it's for you to decide. Whatever it is, it doesn't have to fit inside the box, and it doesn't have to have a label or a definition. For me, it's a deep sense of peace, faith, and freedom without trying to control everything. In the end, spirituality will be your experience, no matter what we call it.

"We are not human beings having a spiritual experience. We are spiritual beings having a human experience."
— Often attributed to Pierre Teilhard de Chardin

Example

I was working on this chapter and was struggling to find an example. Well, I checked my email, and there was a message from someone who read page 111 of a book I co-authored, and told me what it meant to her, and how she also lost her husband 12 years ago, and my overall message was inspiring.

Well, for me, that is not a coincidence. The fact that exactly today, in this chapter, someone took the time to send that email, well, I believe there is definitely something greater than myself who first brought her to that book, gave her the inspiration and message she needed, and today sent me that email.

I guess that is the God of my understanding showing me what example to use.

Think About It: *Have you ever experienced something that felt like more than just a coincidence, like a sign or message meant just for you?*

Ask Yourself

> ➢ How might my life be different if I allowed more peace into my life and were open to discovering what spirituality means to me?

TRUTH: 15

Stop Taking Things Personally

> **"Don't take anything personally. Nothing others do is because of you."**
> — Don Miguel Ruiz (*The Four Agreements*)

Younger Self: *Yes, I pretended to laugh, but honestly, I swear, it feels like every little thing they do is just to get under my skin. Honestly, I'm pretty sure my friend is just fluffing me off lately; everything feels so fake. I can't help but take it personally, like it doesn't matter what I do. They think it's my fault.*

"The Shattering Truths I Wish My Younger Self Knew:

I get it, I spent so much time obsessing over what other people thought of me, especially if I made a mistake or did something embarrassing, I figured they would hold it against me or remember it basically for the rest of my life!

*One other person would treat me a certain way, or give me their opinion, I thought their view of me was true. But this is the biggest truth there is. **Nobody is thinking about you as much as you think.** They have their own lives, and that's what they're focusing on. And their opinions and the way they treat you are not about you! It's* *about their own feelings, beliefs, insecurities, and maybe jealousy. Maybe they were treated a certain way and are taking it out on you. Again, it's not about you. It's about them! You stop yourself from putting yourself out there, doing what you really want to do, because of the fear of what other people might think! Or you make up this story that their actions are all about you. Think about it. Your boss, who usually checks in with you, walks right by. Suddenly, your mind starts spinning: "I just know she's going to remember every mistake I made and hold it against me in my performance review!" But here's the thing, maybe your boss had a fight with her husband, or was in a bad mood and didn't even notice you, it was about what was going on in her life. Now think about a time when you may have had something on your mind and walked past someone whom you usually stop to chat with, but weren't in the mood. It wasn't about them; it was about you! So the next time someone puts you down or disagrees with you, try simply saying, "I'm sorry you feel that way," and then walk away. Leave it with them, don't take it with you. If someone doesn't return a text or ignores you, let them.*

Here are a few tips to try:

- *Don't assume intentions – You can't know why someone said or did something.*
- *Separate facts from feelings – Focus on the situation, not your emotions about it.*
- *Keep in mind their mood – If they're upset, it might not be about you at all.*
- *Choose compassion – Try to see things from their point of view.*

Don't start making up stories of what you did wrong. It is only about them. You will feel drained, stressed, and tired the more you give your power away to people's opinions, behavior; it will never make you feel better. So take your power and energy back, and let go of the expectations you have of other people to act or be a certain way. You will save yourself years of wasted time and stress!

The only thing you're responsible for is how you treat yourself and others. That will be your legacy.

"Don't take anything personally. Nothing others do is because of you. What others say and do is a projection of their own reality, their own dream."

This quote emphasizes that when we take things personally, we allow someone else's perspective to shape our own sense of self. It's a powerful reminder to stay grounded in our own truth.
– Don Miguel Ruiz

Example

"At least I wasn't alone!" I thought when my friend Sally told me this story that I basically did the same thing, except it consisted of jalapeno peppers, burning mouth, and bread for dessert, but I can laugh at it now."

It was the first time Sally had her boyfriend's parents over, and she wanted to impress them with a homemade meal.

She made lasagna a couple of times and thought that would be perfect. Both her parents and her boyfriend's parents were there.

Sally was excited as she waited for everyone to eat. "Don't add any more salt, it's a bit salty." Her mother said. Sally felt her face getting red. All she could think was, "They are going to think I'm an awful cook! Why would my mother point that out?"

The night ended, and her boyfriend said how good everything was. "Yeah, except I'm a horrible cook! I mean, the lasagna was super salty!" "It was a bit salty, but that's because of the recipe, not you as a cook! And the comment was made so people wouldn't add extra salt. You're taking this so personally!"

"How could I not? It is personal! I'm the one who made it!" Sally said as she went through the rest.

After she calmed down, she received a message from her

boyfriend's parents saying how great of a night they had and thanking her for all her work making the delicious dinner, especially the dessert.

She thought about the night, and yes, maybe she overreacted. The lasagna might have been a bit salty, but she rocked the dessert! "I guess I'm not the terrible cook like I said I was. I didn't have to take one thing so personally."

Think About It: Have you ever had your feelings hurt so badly because you took something personally?

Ask Yourself

> ➤ Think about a time you took something personally, and now look at it with a new perspective.

TRUTH: 16

Time Is Never Guaranteed and Health Is Never Promised

"Take care of your body. It's the only place you have to live."
– Jim Rohn

Younger self: *It feels like time is going so slowly! I have ages to figure things out. It's not like anything's gonna happen for a while, so why stress? There's plenty of time to take care of that stuff later when it actually matters.*

The Shattering Truths I Wish My Younger Self Knew:

I will start off with the truth you need to hear. Time is something you will never get back, and health is never guaranteed. Time is often taken for granted, we keep thinking there's plenty of time to do what we really want or enjoy the things we have. So we let time slip through our fingers. Our health can slip just as quickly. In an instant, you can go from being healthy to having an accident or an illness that will change your life.

You can do all the right things, and still, struggle with your health. The part we often forget is that we must take care of both our body and our mind. Yes, life will happen, and you will be disappointed, but there may be something deeper that's going on. It can affect your psychological health. It's so easy to get caught up in the pressure of looking good and chasing money and relationships, but when something doesn't go as planned, everything can crash, and we end up getting depressed and stuck. OK, this is a hard truth: there might not be time to fix broken relationships, chase our dreams, or stop the chances of getting sick. But this is a reminder to live life fully, enjoy it, and make good habits starting now with your health. The truth is, everything is temporary, but you have the power to change the possible outcomes so you can appreciate the time you have right now and feel good. Don't take any of this for granted. But every moment lost to poor health, both physically or mentally, is time we can never buy back.

Back when I was a child, I couldn't wait to grow up, I couldn't wait until I was a teenager and got my license. I couldn't wait till I was older and had my first love. I couldn't wait to graduate and get that job after all those years and all those long nights with extra coffee, but now it's finally over! You see, I couldn't wait to get married; I thought it would be all date nights, but it became more about what we had to do to get the house we wanted, what chores we were going to do, and saving up for everything. I watched people with children and couldn't wait to have my own baby. I finally did, and I couldn't wait until the first time they said mama and actually knew who I was. I couldn't wait to take them on play dates with other moms. I knew it would be so amazing. But the surprising thing was that life was like a juggling act. Between keeping up my relationship, caring for a child, and at the same time, wanting my career to flourish, I couldn't wait until things got easier. Now that I'm a little bit older, I look back and wonder when I started losing touch with friends and family. Where did the time go? I realize everybody else had their own families and their own worlds. Some travel the world, others travel for sporting events. So, I want to remind you that life isn't a race; there's no hurry to get to the end.

"Lost time is never found again, and no promise secures our health for tomorrow. In every challenge and triumph of the day, we learn that both time and our well-being are blessings to be cherished. Let each choice you make be a wise investment in the legacy of your future, acknowledging that the most certain investment is the care of your own life today."
– Benjamin Franklin

Example

Lena was staring at the ceiling, counting the dots on the panels in the hospital room. She used to love going out, but sometimes, she couldn't keep up with the workload of school and her job. She had to get a good grade to get into her dream college.

Her vision started becoming blurry, and she started having headaches. Everyone chalked it up to stress. She needed the money, so she got a job, but not a part-time job, a full-time one! Trying to juggle everything started to weigh heavily on her. Her mom said, "You don't need to do so much, there are still 2 years before you apply to school."

"Well, I can't wait that long, so I'm going to start now! I can't wait to graduate. Things will be so much easier," Lena said. More and more, she started sleeping less. "I'll catch up on sleep next week." Then, one day, she was on her way to school when she noticed her hands were trembling. "I'll make that doctor's appointment during our break."

When she walked into school, she felt weak, and her whole body shook. She fell and hit her head. She was having a seizure. She was rushed to the hospital, and they said she also had a concussion. "We have to keep you here for tests and monitoring."

As she lay in that bed, she realized that she had ignored all her symptoms purely to get ahead. She was lying in that hospital bed, staring at the clock, and thought to herself, "I've wasted so much time. I could've spent sleeping, hanging out with my family, or just living my life. I thought I had all the time in the world, that my health would always be fine as long as I kept chasing my dreams. But now, everything was on hold."

She realized now that there was no race, and that both her time and her health were fragile, something she had taken for granted.

Think About It: *Have you ever pushed yourself too hard trying to reach a goal, only to suffer burnout?*

Ask Yourself

> ➤ *What is one small change you can make now that you realize the value of time and health?*

TRUTH: 17

Grieving the Life You Thought You'd Have

> *"Grief is not something you complete, but rather, you endure. Grief is not a task to finish and move on, but an element of yourself—an alteration of your being."* — Gwen Flowers

Younger self: *Why is everyone telling me, 'Don't worry, you will feel better soon'? I mean, I just went through a huge loss; no one will understand. Heck, I don't even understand! I want to crawl into bed and never come out!*

The Shattering Truth I Wish My Younger Self Knew:

Grief is something that is personal, and everyone deals with it differently. Some people might feel really sad, and someone else might get angry or even act like everything's okay. The truth is, it is important to remember that it doesn't matter how someone grieves; it's okay, and there's no right or wrong way to feel.

And I'm not only talking about mourning a loved one, but it can be anyone or anything that meant something to you in your life, even pets. It can be a dream or a whole part of your identity. You may ask, "Who am I now?" Not only after losing a loved one, but maybe after losing a job for any reason, being fired, laid off, or being sick.

I have a rare disease, so I have to grieve some of the limitations I was once able to do. Grief isn't something that you "get over." It is something that you live with and becomes a part of you, the new you. There are stages of grief that any book or search will tell you. They are;

- *Denial*
- *Anger*
- *Bargaining*
- *Depression*
- *Acceptance.*

For me, I bounced, skipped, and sometimes dove headfirst around each one several times. But here's a shattering truth: grief is not something you need to fix. It's not a puzzle to be solved, and there's no perfect way to grieve. What you need the most is space to feel, to cry, to be angry, or even to let yourself laugh. It's OK if you start to feel like you're unraveling because that's when you will find the strength to rebuild. After any loss, it may change you, but it does not define you. Give yourself some time to have patience and grace. It will take time, but the pieces will start to align again, and you will realize that grief, while painful, will also open up space for growth and a new resilience you never thought you had. It's getting back up even when you don't want to. It's that quiet strength to embrace life as it is right now.

"Grief is in two parts. The first is loss. The second is the remaking of life." — Anne Roiphe

Example

One minute, Jordan and Eli were joking over FaceTime. The next, Eli was gone. A car accident. No warning. No goodbye.

Now Jordan keeps checking his phone, hoping for a message that won't come. At school, people glance at him, then quickly look away. No one knows what to say. His teachers ask if he's okay, but he quietly changes the subject. He starts skipping lunch, then practice. He avoids the hallways where they used to walk together. The music they shared, the jokes they had, even the silence between them everything reminds him of Eli.

One night, Jordan rides his bike to the park where they used to meet. He sits on their bench, staring at the empty space beside him. He stays there for hours. Maybe hoping for a sign. Maybe just needing to feel close to something that used to feel safe. Nothing feels real. Nothing feels right. And he doesn't know if it ever will again.

And that's okay. Because grief doesn't follow the rules. There's no checklist, no straight path. Some days might feel numb. Others might feel unbearable. Some days you might laugh and then feel guilty for it. Other days you might cry without even knowing why. All of it is human. All of it is normal, even when it doesn't feel like it.

Think About It: *Have you experienced any loss where it feels as if no one understands you?*

Ask Yourself

Where in my life do I have to grieve?

TRUTH: 18

Manifesting Starts with Believing, Not Begging

> *"Act as if what you intend to manifest is already a reality.*
> *That which you are seeking is seeking you."* — Wayne Dyer

Younger Self: *I have been wishing for a million dollars, but I'm broke! I can almost see myself driving a fancy car in my mansion, but that's just wishful thinking.*

The Shattering Truths I Wish My Younger Self Knew:

Manifesting is getting clear on what you want and aligning yourself to attract it. This isn't just about thinking happy thoughts or crossing your fingers and hoping for the best. It's about stepping into a different mindset, one that's grounded in abundance, not in fear or lack. Instead of saying, "I don't want to be broke," try something like, "Money finds its way to me in expected and unexpected ways." The key is to speak from the reality you want to live, not the one you're trying to escape. The main idea is to notice if you have any blockages. For example, you might think you want a promotion at work, but deep down, you are afraid of the extra work. So first, getting clear, you might be thinking of your dream car, but take it further. Do you want to have your dream car? Or do you want to be driving your dream car? So first, be very clear and specific, and write it down. Feel as if you already have it. Step into that new reality. Use all your senses. What do you see, smell, feel, taste, and hear?

Bring your vibration up, or you can say, get into a state of happiness, joy, and bliss. Feel excitement every time you think of this. Let go of the need to control exactly how things will unfold. When opportunities present themselves, take action. That's when the next step will show up faster than you can say, "I didn't see that coming." Before you know it, you'll be a magnet for your deepest desires.

Believe wholeheartedly that the Universe is working with you and for you, not against you. This is not wishful thinking; it is bringing exactly what you want into your life. You have to let go of any doubt; you have to fully believe that you are receiving it. Here are a couple of techniques that you can implementing today!

"*You become what you believe.*" – Oprah Winfrey

Here is a quick recap of some steps, but try some new ones that work for you, because it will work!

- *Get Clear on What You Want: Be specific what you want to manifest.*
- *Feel it: Close your eyes and imagine yourself already having it. Visualize it as if it's happening right now.*
- *Affirmations: Use positive statements like, "I am worthy of this," or "This is already on its way to me."*
- *Let Go: Trust that it can happen. Let go of doubts and believe that the universe is on your side.*
- *Take Inspired Action: Do things that feel right or opportunities that come your way. Manifestation isn't just about thinking; it's also about acting.*
- *Gratitude: Be thankful for what you already have, and the universe will bring you more.*

- *Make a vision board, or write/draw what you will attract*

These are simple steps, but they work when you stay consistent and positive!

I made a vision board and went above and beyond even what I thought I wanted. I wanted to write a book, so I took a picture of myself holding "my book." I wrote Amazon's number one bestseller on it. I only believed that it would be done. People, places, and things came into my life at this exact time, and it took work on my part. Yes, I had to write it. And in the end, I did write my book, which became Amazon's number-one bestseller! So now, what do you really want? Be sure to state it positively. Feel the excitement that you're finally making up your mind and receiving it. Now let go of the control and enjoy the process of having it in your life!

Another technique comes from Neville Goddard, who identified a powerful moment when manifestation is at its highest: the state just before you fall asleep. It's that space where you're not fully awake, yet not completely asleep—a window into your subconscious mind when it's most impressionable and open to suggestion.

This is the perfect time to focus on the reality you want to create. After all, you're going to sleep anyway—why let your final thoughts be stressful or negative? Instead, let them center around your ultimate vision. When you do, your mind continues working on that reality while you sleep.

"If, as you prepare for sleep, you do not consciously feel yourself into the state of the answered wish, then you will take the sum total of the reactions and feelings of the waking day, and while asleep you'll be instructed in the manner in which they'll be expressed tomorrow." —Neville Goddard

So, deliberately rehearse what you want. Let your thoughts flow freely, and allow yourself to feel the excitement of already having

it—while resting in a peaceful state. It might sound simple, but your mind has been conditioned to drift into worry. With practice, you can train it to focus on joy, clarity, and intention instead. Smile, concentrate on what you want, and over time, you'll begin to change your mental habits—and watch your desired reality begin to manifest.

"What you think, you create. What you feel, you attract. What you imagine, you become." — Buddha

Example

This reminds me of a friend who is now a professor. Mia was a teenager who had been feeling stuck, started reading a book about manifesting. At first, she thought it was just wishful thinking, but as time went on, she remembered how many times she was focused on something or somewhere she wanted to go, and she was already manifesting!

She took some time and let her mind daydream. Her brother walked in and asked, "What are you doing?" Mia replied, "Manifesting! I'm manifesting working at the college." She was already acting, and instead of being a student, she was acting like a professor! "Yeah right, good luck with that, your grades suck." Her brother said.

She continued reading, felt the ground where she was walking, and heard her voice teaching science. You see, Mia had always loved science, but she struggled with her grades. The next day, she was on her phone, not paying attention to where she was going, and she accidentally went into the wrong class. "Oh, sorry," she said as she was leaving. "Wait!" said a senior student. "We are having a study group, and we need to have at least 15 people, or else they won't give us the classroom. Is there any way you would like to join?" Immediately, she knew this was meant to be. "Yes, I am having a difficult time in science." "Perfect," said the young man, "science was my best subject!"

Mia stayed in the study group through the rest of her schooling, and more students joined. She found herself helping other students!

As she continued to follow her passion, one of the professors asked her if she would like to work with him on an additional project. "Yes!" she said. It might not be her dream, but she was on her way and felt empowered. And I guess I spoiled the outcome in the beginning. Yes, she did become a professor, maybe not the way she thought, but the way it was meant to happen.

Think About It: *Have you stopped yourself from letting yourself dream of what you want because you were convinced that it wouldn't matter?*

Ask Yourself

> ➢ What would I love to have? Then, picture every detail about it and feel happy about achieving it. Be grateful.

TRUTH: 19

E.I-From Frustration to Freedom: How to Break the Cycle

> **"Most folks are about as happy as they make up their minds to be."** — Abraham Lincoln

Younger Self: *Emotional intelligence? OK, I get it. You don't like it when I flip out. It's just sometimes people are so dramatic. Oh, and what am I supposed to do when someone totally insults me?*

The Shattering Truths I Wish My Younger Self Knew:

Emotional intelligence (E.I.) is basically about being aware of how you're feeling and then having the ability to actually pause and think before reacting. It's also understanding how others are feeling and then knowing how to respond appropriately. Honestly, I wish they had taught this in school because it would have helped me at any age. It's taking some time to pause and check in to see how you're feeling. Are you about to blow up or get upset over something that's totally out of your control? When you're aware of this, it influences everything: how you cope with stress, deal with conflicts, and even your health! It's like the secret sauce to your life—if you don't get it right, things might just taste a little bitter.

Another big part of E.I. is empathy, which is trying to see things from someone else's perspective. When you're paying attention to your emotions, you can actually catch yourself when you're feeling angry, jealous, or resentful, and you can work on shifting these feelings towards feeling something more positive. The problem you think you have isn't the problem. It's the way you react that is the problem.

Here are some ways to practice emotional intelligence:

- *Breathe deeply. Pause, inhale slowly, and exhale to calm your mind.*
- *Check your thoughts. Identify negative self-talk and replace it with a positive, realistic perspective.*
- *Label your emotions. Name what you're feeling to gain clarity and control.*
- *Practice empathy. Try to understand others' feelings before reacting.*
- *Pause before reacting. Take a moment to respond thoughtfully rather than impulsively.*
- *Be mindful of body language. Your body reflects your emotions—adjust it to match what you want to feel.*

Small adjustments like these can help strengthen your Emotional Intelligence and improve your overall emotional state!

Now, it's up to you how to bring yourself to a place of happiness and peace. For me, it's dancing, music, singing in the shower, walking in nature, meditating, and so many other things. There's no right way or wrong way to do it. The most important thing is recognizing your feelings and then taking action. Now, I'm not saying you always have to feel good. If you need to cry, then cry. If you feel sad, that's OK too, but don't let yourself get stuck there because it's so easy to spiral down, and it becomes harder to raise your emotions to a place where you can manage them. This is a skill we're not born with; we have to learn it, and when you keep working towards feeling positive, your life will be more peaceful. One example is jumping in your car on your way to an important meeting, but getting stopped by a train, causing a traffic jam. Now you can feel irritated and let frustration take over how you feel, but ask yourself, is this serving me? Is it going to make the train go any faster and clear up the traffic? That's when you can have the control to shift it, and instead of getting all worked up, you can use that time to relax, do whatever helps, maybe listen to some calm music, take deep breaths, or do car karaoke. Remember, you're the only one who's responsible for how you react despite what's going on. Now, think about it. How are you feeling right now? How do you want to feel now? Strive for that? The more you practice this, the easier it becomes, and trust me, your future self will thank you.

"When dealing with people, remember you are not dealing with creatures of logic, but creatures of emotion."
— Dale Carnegie

Example

It was a rainy afternoon when Josh rushed inside, soaked through. "You've got to be kidding me! I can't believe I have to be wet all day," he mumbled, clearly annoyed. Everyone else was just as drenched, but no one seemed to make it a big deal. Later, during a group project, Tim suggested an idea that Josh didn't quite agree with. Without thinking, Josh blurted out, "That's ridiculous. You finally speak up, and this is the best you've got?" The words came out before he could stop them, and the whole group went dead quiet. Tim looked down, avoiding eye contact, and the rest of the group suddenly found their shoes really interesting.

Josh immediately regretted what he'd said. He wasn't a bad guy, just someone who had a bad habit of speaking without thinking. Tim didn't seem too eager to hear an apology, and Josh could practically feel the awkwardness hanging in the air. As the day went on, he realized how easily his careless words had pushed everyone away.

He wished he could've taken a second to just pause before reacting, kind of like having a piece of tape to cover his mouth. Instead, all he could feel was the uncomfortable silence that followed. Later, he pulled Tim aside and, with a sigh, said, "Hey, sorry about earlier. I didn't mean to come off like that." Tim gave him a half-smile and replied, "It's fine. Just think next time." Josh nodded, feeling a little better but still wishing he'd handled it better. He realized how important the saying, "think before you speak," or "pause and ask yourself W.A.I.T: Why Am I Talking? Really was!

Think About It: *What is something that causes you to react and lose control of your emotions?*

Ask Yourself

> ➢ What's one strategy you can use to pause and think before reacting?

TRUTH: 20

Authentic: Unapologetically You

"Be yourself; everyone else is already taken. Authenticity is the most powerful tool you have. Embrace who you are, flaws and all, because that's what makes you truly unique."

— Inspired by Oscar Wilde

Younger Self: *Let me be honest, people like who they expect me to be, and I'm ok with that. It makes it easier because I don't have to be afraid of being judged. You can't possibly understand how much pressure it takes to fit in and act "normal." I overthink every detail, what others expect of me, so I lose connection with who I truly am. Maybe that's what happens when you grow up.*

The Shattering Truths I Wish My Younger Self Knew:

Being authentic means embracing who you truly are, quirks and all, without pretending to be anyone else. It's about showing up as your real self and feeling good in your own skin. Take this challenge. Ask yourself, if I knew that you wouldn't face any negative consequences for my behaviors, how would you show up?

- *What would you wear?*
- *How would you speak?*
- *How would you behave?*

- *How would you decorate your space?*
- *What color of car would you really want (fluorescent Pink?), or would it be a monster truck?*
- *Would you lie about your age?*
- *Would you hang art on your wall that makes you laugh, even if it confuses your guests?*
- *Would you throw a birthday party for your dog with a full guest list and cake? (don't judge!)*

Answer these questions without judging if your answers are "good" or "bad." It takes tremendous courage to strip away the layers of who the world says you should be. I know that it can feel paralyzing to worry about being accepted. It's like you've worn a mask for so long that taking it off is vulnerable, exposing others to see the real you.

"When I was 5 years old, my mother always told me that happiness was the key to life. When I went to school, they would ask me what I wanted to do when I grew up. I wrote down "happy". They told me I didn't understand the assignment, and I told them they didn't understand life." — John Lennon

The key is accepting yourself fully. First, give yourself permission to follow your passion. It also shifts in different situations but still holds the same values. From experience, yes, you might lose friends, but why do you want them in your life anyway? You will inspire others to share how they want to live, and you will find your tribe. Now, you deserve the kind of peace that you will feel when you don't have to pretend and the freedom that comes with it. You will learn a new level of happiness, and remember, no matter how messy, imperfect, or out of place you feel, that is what makes you extraordinary. This will be an ah-ha moment that will leave you wondering, "Do they like me?" to asking, "Do I like who I am?"

"Authenticity is the daily practice of letting go of who we think we're supposed to be and embracing who we are."
— Brene Brown

Example

Luke sat on the edge of his bed, flipping through the small stack of cash he'd managed to save over the past few months. It definitely wasn't a fortune, but it was just enough to finally get himself a halfway decent car. His current ride was holding on by a thread, and every time he saw his friends roll up in their shiny, new cars with touchscreens and backup cameras, a tiny knot twisted in his stomach.

He wasn't even a car guy. Never had been. But lately, it felt like everyone around him had it all figured out. And he... didn't.

What really stung was overhearing some of his friends one night. They were laughing at someone from their old high school who still drove a beat-up sedan. "Can you imagine showing up in *that* thing?" someone blurted out. Everyone laughed. Luke forced a chuckle, but it hit him harder than he let on.

The next week, after scrolling through listings and comparing prices, he pulled the trigger. The car wasn't anything special; it was used, but it looked decent enough. He drained his savings to make it happen. Not because he loved the car, but because he couldn't stand the idea of being judged.

When he pulled up to hang out that weekend, one of the guys slapped the roof and grinned. "You finally decided to join the human race with a *real car*," Luke laughed, and for a moment, he felt good, even a bit proud.

But that feeling didn't last.

The next thing he knew, a rock hit his windshield, and a crack grew like a spider web. He pulled over, staring at it, and just sat there.

"This isn't even the car I wanted," he muttered under his breath.

A few days later, an ad popped up online: a heavily discounted trip to a place he'd dreamed of visiting for years. A real adventure. But he couldn't even consider it because the money was gone, spent on a car that didn't mean anything to him. Frustration sank in like a weight on his chest.

And that's when it hit him.

He hadn't bought the car for himself. Not really. He bought it because he felt like he *had* to. Because the fear of being left out, laughed at, or looked down on was louder than his own voice. And now, here he was, missing out on something that actually mattered to him.

That night, Luke made himself a promise: no more chasing after things just to look good to other people. No more ignoring what *he* actually wanted.

Because at the end of the day, real success isn't about shiny cars or fitting in. It's about living a life that feels good on the inside, even if it doesn't always look flashy on the outside.

Think About It: *Has there been a time when you made choices, acted, or dressed like others, even though you wished you could just be yourself?*

Ask Yourself

> ➤ If I knew that you wouldn't face any negative consequences for my behaviors, what I wore, where I would work, what I would love to do how would you show up?

TRUTH: 21

Your Purpose Isn't a Job Title

> *Every day we consciously or unconsciously fulfill our purpose by simply being ourselves and sharing our unique gifts with the world to make a difference in the lives of those around us.*

Younger Self: *It feels like everyone has their purpose, but I'm just still trying to figure out if I have one! I haven't done anything big or saved anyone. I mean, it's not like whatever I do is going to make a difference! It hasn't yet, so when will I know when this magical time will be? Is it in my job? It's so confusing, and I don't want to even get my hopes up, only to be let down.*

The Shattering Truths I Wish My Younger Self Knew:

You see, your purpose isn't one thing; it can be based on many things. You are fulfilling your purpose each and every day. It is hard to believe you do not have to "find" your purpose, because simply being born, you already have a purpose in this world. The purpose isn't some huge, impossible thing; it's found in the simple gestures. It's when you hold the door open for someone struggling with their hands full, and their relieved smile reminds you that you made a difference.

The purpose isn't about grand achievements; it's in the everyday choices. For example, when you send an encouraging message to a friend who is having a rough day, and they text back, "I really needed that." Maybe you ran back and picked up a necklace that someone dropped, even though it meant you had to hurry to your next class or job. You have no idea how much sentimental value it meant to that person. Your purpose might not be what you do for a living but how you show up in the little moments. I know you've been on this search to find your purpose, thinking it has to be something life-altering, something that will make you stand out. You might have imagined it as a big event, like winning an award or getting a huge round of applause. You've been waiting for that one moment of clarity that will reveal exactly what you're meant to do as if the purpose is a place you'll eventually arrive at. You don't find your purpose somewhere else. You create your purpose exactly where you are and give meaning to it.

Here are everyday ways to fulfill your purpose:

- *Practice Kindness: Whether it's a smile, a compliment, or a helping hand, small acts of kindness create ripple effects that align with a greater purpose.*
- *Engage in Meaningful Conversations: Share your insights, listen deeply, and uplift others through the power of connection.*
- *Be Present in the Moment: Purpose isn't just found in big achievements; it's in the way you fully show up for each experience, whether it's washing dishes or having a heart-to-heart conversation with a friend.*
- *Take Inspired Action: Even if it's a small step, do something daily that moves you closer to living your purpose, whether it's journaling, creating, or learning.*
- *Leave Every Interaction Better Than You Found It – Whether through encouragement, wisdom, or simply being fully present, make every encounter a reflection of your purpose.*

Your purpose is to take care of yourself, fight through the hard times, take care of your body, and get help when you need it. It's about living out your life using your gifts and talents instead of dismissing them or trying to be like someone else. You make a difference. The most important part is that you usually fulfill your purpose without even knowing it, but you have impacted someone's life more than you could imagine. Leave this world better than you found it!

"The purpose of life is not to be happy. It is to be useful, to be honorable, to be compassionate, to have it make some difference that you have lived and lived well." — Ralph Waldo Emerson

Example

John sat on his bed, scrolling through social media, watching all his friends brag about the school they got into or the amazing job. John felt lost; he had no idea what he was going to do with his life or what his purpose was.

That weekend, there was a concert that they had paid for tickets to three months ago. John jumped in the car to pick up his friends who were going to a concert when this dog darted out. He quickly stopped and made sure the dog was ok. The dog was scared and very friendly, so he knew it was a pet.

He was able to see a phone number on his collar as his friends were texting him, "Hurry up, we'll be late for the concert!" He said I found this dog.....and his friends kept saying, "Who cares?" John stopped taking the messages and called the number. "Hello?" Said a lady. "Hi, my name is John, and I think I have your dog." He heard her start to cry. "Her name is Hope, and she is my daughter's service dog! We've been looking for her for 2 days!" He found that he was almost across the city. "I'll bring her back," John said after she gave him her address.

His friends were messaging like crazy, and the last one was, "If you're not here in the next 5 minutes, we're leaving." John arrived at the lady's house, where this teary-eyed teen daughter was, and just hugged Hope. "Please come in," she begged. He felt so grateful, he sent a message to his friends, "Go ahead, something more important came up." And he sat at the table while they both told the story of how he got lost and then John said he almost hit her. "You're an earth angel!" John said, "No, I'm just happy I was able to help out."

"You don't understand what this means to us!" Said the lady as she tried to give him money. "I can't take it. I guess there was a reason why I was there at that time." She quickly interrupted and said, "No, it was your purpose."

That night, his phone blew up with pictures of his friends at the concert, but he didn't have an ounce of remorse. He thought about that day and realized that finding that dog was his purpose that day. It didn't have to be getting into a certain school or job; it was in everyday things.

Think About It: *Can you remember when you intentionally did something nice for another person just because it felt right?*

Ask Yourself

> ➢ Where can you find a moment of purpose in an ordinary day—not something big, but something that made a difference to someone else?

TRUTH: 22

Now Are The Memories We Make For Tomorrow

> *"We do not remember days, we remember moments."*
> — Cesare Pavese

Younger Self: *I have so much to juggle. I don't even remember what having fun means! I definitely will make time tomorrow to visit some people right after I get through my to-do list. Now, I can't remember all the things I have to do!*

The Shattering Truths I Wish My Younger Self Knew:

Memories are made right now, and what kind are up to you? It's easy to get caught up in life, and we forget to make people and fun a priority. Let me give you an example.

My Mimi had a teacup collection, and when she passed away, they were all distributed among her kids. My mind raced back to the times I would be at her house when she unfolded the TV tray, specifically the one with different flowers all over it. She would make us tea, and yes, for an 8-year-old, this was still special. When there were bubbles on top, she would say, "Quick, eat those, it means money!" We would tell stories, and she treated me as an equal, not a kid. I have some of those teacups, not because of their worth but because their meaning is priceless. I still have a cup of tea in them, think of stories, and laugh, knowing her love is with me, with the memories I cherish. It's those random jokes, unexpected conversations, or even awkward moments that turn into the stories you'll look back on and smile about.

Possessions don't give you that. The stuff will be gone, even the tea cups, but so will the people, and you can't put a price tag on memories. As we grow up, one day, our grandkids will walk into our house, look at the pictures on the wall, and ask what it was like growing up. How will you answer? One day, your great-great-grandchildren will see those pictures fading, replaced with newer ones of different generations. One day, the car you worked so hard for will be towed away for scrap, rusted and forgotten. One day, the house you live in will be sold, torn down, or remodeled by a stranger. One day, your name may no longer be spoken. Your face may not be remembered. One day, you'll look back and realize all the things you planned to do "one day" never happened. You were waiting for the right time to travel, to spend more time with family, to pursue your passion. But time ran out. Because in the end, you can't take the money, the possessions, or the status with you. All that remains is the love you gave and the memories you made that will be passed on.

"Sometimes you will never know the value of a moment, until it becomes a memory." – Dr. Seuss

Example

It was a sunny afternoon, and Allie went shopping for her prom dress. After trying on a lot of dresses, her mom lit up as she walked out with the perfect one.

After, they went for lunch. She asked her mom all sorts of questions about her prom. They took their time, even shared a dessert, and laughed at the styles of the dress and the best part was her hairstyle! Allie ended up learning so many things about her mom; she saw her differently and felt a stronger connection.

When they came home, Allie's dad said, "Well, you guys were out all afternoon; it must have been exhausting!" Allie smiled and said, "Actually, no, it was a great afternoon!" Her mom went to put her coat away, and before Allie ran to call her friends, she gave her mom a big hug and said, "Thank you." Her mom said, "Of course, that is the perfect dress!" Allie replied, "No, not just the dress, but about the whole day."

This wasn't about a dress she was going to wear one day; it was a dress that would provide memories for both of them for many years.

Think About It: *Do you have a memory that has nothing to do with possession but with a person?*

Ask Yourself

> ➢ What memory can you create today that your future self will thank you for?

Conclusion - well not really it's just the beginning!

Beware the *"life has to be so hard!"* Myth. Mind-blowing right? And that's what I wish my younger self knew before I was in pain and fear for too long.

After you start applying these **22 truths** you will see the transformation, your attitude will change and your soul will start to heal in ways you never dreamed it could.

Guess what? I wish I could tell you that you will wake up tomorrow with **more time**, so you get to decide if you want to make the most of today's learnings.

Sure, I could give you one of these easy fluffy endings but let's get real, that's just not how life goes. If you've learned anything from these pages, it's that life is messy and erratic but beautiful and imperfect.

I've told you barely half of what I've ever known, and I'm sure you've got some life-changing secrets to tell me.

Let's start shattering them because you've got this! There's something about the knowledge that you know is true and it is **not a coincidence** that you read this book today, right now.

After some laughs, some tears, and mostly ah-ha moments, there is no need to waste time and get to be the person you were created to be with **Shattering Truths I Wish My Younger Self Knew!**

The Truths I Learned From Living Life

I asked 111 people what life advice would they give their younger self, or advice they now want to share.

111 List:

1. *"For people to be kind. Shine Brightly"*

Howard Brown,

USA

2. *"Everything that happens in life is divinely orchestrated to help you fulfill your soul's mission. The light of your true essence can only be revealed in your darkest moments, so trust the process, put your faith in the creator, and watch miracles unfold around you!"*

Tina Brigley

Ontario, Canada

tinabrigleycoaching@gmail.com

3. *"Your story is like chapters in a book. Don't get stuck re-reading an old chapter, it won't change, no matter how many times you read it.*

Keep turning the page, the best chapter might just be about to unfold."

Jacqueline Cadger,

Stonehaven, Scotland

betterlifebelievers@gmail.com

4. *"You are stronger than you know and wiser than you realize. Never forget to love yourself fully and fiercely. You are enough— exactly as you are—and so deeply worthy of all the beauty, love, and magic this life has to offer. Keep believing in yourself, keep showing up with love, and trust that your light is meant to shine."*

Sanet Van Breda

Johannesburg, South Africa

slim@selflove4me.com

5. *"こんにちは、*

クリスタ・ローズ。

私はクリスです。

初めまして

Don't be afraid to try new things, to learn new things. Embrace your uniqueness."

Chris

Tokyo Japan

6. *"Take chances and when given an opportunity, take it, even if it is out of your comfort zone."*

Sarah Parsons,

Rochester NY

northcoastconsulting@outlook.com

7. *"Work on yourself to change the World. It's an inside job."*

Francesca Lucia

Ontario, Canada

francescalucia111@gmail.com

8. *"Never cry over a mistake. They are life's way of teaching us how to rise, not reasons to fall. Pause before speaking in anger; silence can be wiser than words you'll wish you could take back. Never sleep mad at the one you love; connection matters more than ego. You're not losing people or opportunities, you're making space. Trust that what's meant for you won't need chasing. Let people reveal who they are, then act accordingly. Not everyone holds the same intentions as you do. protect your light. And finally, don't fear the unknown. Every new door is a possibility waiting to bless you. Walk through boldly."*

The Legendary Coach Eve

Scotland

coacheve3@gmail.com

9. *"Always stay the course no matter what."*

Michael Barry

Ontario, Canada

Barry.michael.p@gmail.com

10. *"Advice to my younger self: Look hard in each difficult situation you face and find the lesson you need to learn from it. Each lesson will build you up to be the Badass, Beautiful QUEEN you are meant to become in the Future."*

Connie Walton-

Ada, OK

Www.Conniewalton.com

11. *"Believe in miracles every day and remind yourself you are one"*

Heather

Ontario, Canada

heathersreiki@gmail.com

12. *"I know you are feeling troubled. Please pause and take a breath for a second. I wish I could sit beside you, look you in the eye, and remind you of this one simple truth: Be true to who you are. Not who you think you should be. Not who others expect. Just... you. That's more than enough. Some days you'll doubt yourself—everyone does. But I promise you, your voice matters. Your story matters. You don't need all the answers right now. Just take the next step. Trust your heart. You're not broken—you're becoming. And that light inside you? It hasn't gone anywhere. Let it shine."*

With love, always—

Anne James

Tasmania, Australia

anne@viphealthmastery.com

13. *"We get once chance at this short and beautiful life. You alone are the director of your life story. So surround yourself with people, places, and things that make you feel safe, lucky, successful, and loved."*

Julie Ann Baxter

Orange County.

14. *"That instinct you are feeling, that whispering voice,*

that clairvoyance of what is happening is real.

Trust it, follow it, nurture it.

This connection to who you really are will

always guide you."

Gail Kraft

Londonderry, NH

kraftingbravery@gmail.com

15. *"My message is that no matter what we going through in life, we need to be thankful and grateful that we are still here alive and that we all have a purpose in life and we need to find it and embrace it."*

Regards,

Vanessa Chetty

From Benoni, Gauteng.

vanessa.chetty0512@gmail.com

16. "Forgiveness is a laser-sharp tool. If it makes you feel smaller and more tense or bigger, better, and above the other, it is not working (hello ego).

If it feels lighter and freeing, you are on the right track."

Christina Heike

NYC, US

info@NewDecisionTherapyNYC.com

17. *"So many people dream of winning the lottery—that life-changing, multimillion-dollar jackpot. But the truth is, most will never see that big prize. All that money spent, time wasted, and energy drained chasing a number… when the real jackpot is you.*

You are the lottery.

That $60 million winning ticket? It's been you all along.

Stop thinking small! Demand more of yourself and watch how the universe conspires in your favour!"

GQ Tarot

Ontario, Canada

gqtarot@gmail.com

18. *"Your intensity isn't too much—it's insight. Your tears weren't weakness—they were training. You're not dramatic. You're discerning."*

Raquel

Chicago, USA

https://yourgpsforsuccess.net/

19. *"Always get back up! There was a time when I was completely bedridden and things seemed hopeless. I was even told that I would never work again or even function. God had another plan, however. Every day, I visualized myself out of that bed, walking and even running. I visualized being with my kids and husband, going to Disney World with them, and traveling the world with them. Vision and faith lead to outcomes. So, please no matter how bleak things seem, never ever give up!"*

Dr. Karen,

Chicago IL.

https://www.thejunipercenter.com/our-staff/n-karen-thames/

20. *"You will spend years giving yourself away in pieces, mistaking being chosen for being safe. You'll call it love, but it will feel like disappearing. One day, in the stillness of your own undoing, you'll hear a voice—soft but certain—that says: Come back. And you will. Not to who you were, but to who you were always becoming."*

– Reem

Ontario, Canada

21. *"Silence is abuse's biggest ally.*

keep speaking up and sharing your story, it will not only help you, I guarantee you, it will help others too!

Today's tears of sorrow water the seeds of joy for tomorrow, but we don't have to wait until tomorrow to feel the joy in today. Get out and play!"

Christianna

Ontario, Canada

https://www.facebook.com/share/12HN551YhwU/

22. *"The most meaningful thing I've learned is, that we all really just want to feel seen no matter our age."*

Shalina Bell,

Rutherford, New Jersey

dreamtovision@gmail.com

23. *"Advice to younger self....Spend more time with mom & dad, listen and ask about family history.*

Go to more family functions instead of putting in extra hours on the business.

Do your work, but enjoy your family, they won't always be here.

Make sure you take care of yourself so you can live a long and productive life.

Spend time with your loved ones sharing stories and having fun.

Every day is a Gift, cherish the day and live in the now."

Michael Crawley

Ontario, Canada

michael@theprofessorofprosperity.com

24. *"Believe in yourself even when it feels uncomfortable—confidence is built through action, not perfection. Don't wait for permission to chase your dreams; go after what you want boldly and unapologetically."*

Alyssa Anderson

Ontario, Canada

alyssa.anderson@dfsin.ca

25. *"The mind needs to be calm to navigate the chaos in life. Learn to meditate and practice it daily."*

Gordon Simms

26. *"If I could whisper one truth to my younger self, it would be this: Happiness isn't something you find — it's something you design, one intentional choice at a time. Care for your Health, hold Affection for yourself, live with Purpose, build strong Partnerships, and stay Youthful at heart. Life will shatter and rebuild you, and please remember, you are always evolving into something stronger."*

Leigh Ann Hello

Ontario, Canada

www.HelloHappiness.ca

27. *"To my younger self, 'Be patient and kind, forgive and love yourself for you are always beautiful, even on your worst days. Look inside, see your light, and ask your heart, not your head. It will always lead to you, most amazingly. And finally, BE LOVE.'"*

Janice Peterson

Windsor, Ontario, Canada

https://www.facebook.com/people/Quantum-Heal-with-Janice

28. *"When you chase your dreams, don't just be the dog that catches the car—be the smart puppy who already knows how to drive it. Manifestation isn't just about calling it in; it's about becoming the person who effortlessly embodies your vision. Step fully into the "YOU" you need to BE, and watch your dreams chase you instead."*

Carole Filion,

Colgan, Ontario | 647-273-5531

29. *"My advice to women in pursuit of excellence is to train yourself to receive and rest well so you don't dim your essence or withhold your truest and best from the people you love and your purpose.*

Practice receiving without Big Pride that says "I don't need it" or Little Pride that says, "I don't deserve it." Practice resting without Guilt or Shame saying, "I need to do more" or "I should." It will require discipline rooted in deep love and when you move in that freedom, your power is channeled and replenished and you will find fulfillment."

Samantha Stewartz

Pennsylvania, USA

stewartzsamantha@gmail.com

30. *"After living in 10 countries and traveling to almost 50, I encourage teenagers to take the leap and go on an exchange program in highschool. When you leave your bubble, your country, then you discover who you truly are and where you come from. It's scary, but what you learn goes way beyond what any classroom in university or college can teach you. Spend more time outside than inside, explore on your feet not on your screen."*

Joanna Dobrzeniecki

Ontario, Canada

biohackyourfamily.com

31. *"Be decisive in all that you do. Life is too short to overthink everything, procrastinate and delay things that can be done today. I have developed the ability to be a massive action taker and feel comfortable making executive decisions quickly. This is an essential skill to develop that can improve one's life both personally and professionally. Life can and should be grand! Live fully alive each day and be courageous to be bold."*

Jose Escobar

Maryland (USA)

www.ConnectedLeadersAcademy.com

32. *"Everything your heart desires begins with faith. Stay true to who you are. Don't let fear steal your peace, your purpose, your happiness. Let your faith guide you—it will always lead you to the path you're meant to walk."*

Giovanna Tartarone,

New York, USA

SparkngChangeWithGigi.com

33. *"PLEASE. Pour into your husband. Pour into your healing. See him as the man who loved you enough to choose you - he wants to be a good husband. He can't do that if you hide your heart from him. Learn how to ask for what you need and want from a place of love and knowing that you get to have it. You are worthy. You are a walking miracle. You are the portal to greatness for your family, and that means you are the one. The one to heal. To ask for what is needed. The one to show up with persistence and LOVE."*

Amanda Miller

Indiana

amandarebeccamiller@gmail.com

34. *"Follow the passion that lights you up — it's the compass of your soul. The dreams that stir your heart were placed there for a reason. Trust them. Even when the path feels uncertain, passion will always illuminate the next step. Your soul already knows the way; you simply have to say yes."*

Edyta France, n.d., Ontario, Canada

www.AscendNow.ca

35. *"The deepest wounds often hold the greatest wisdom. Allow yourself to feel, heal, and rise from your struggles, for it is in embracing your darkness that you'll discover the light within."*

Jane Cordeiro,

Ontario, Canada

36. *"Speak to yourself as you would your best friend. You will hear words of grace, mercy, kindness and forgiveness which develops courage. In time, you'll walk in holy confidence, learning to love the one He is tenderly shaping you to be."*

Heidi Marie Cooksey

Mississippi, Gulf Coast

Heidicooksey@gmail.com

37. *"Find moments to tune into yourself. Be absolutely unafraid to feel what you feel.*

Always choose expression over suppression by nurturing your creative spirit.

You are always in charge of your happiness.

Trust in your own power to change that which is negative into a fuel for your growth,

When they find you 'too this' or 'too that', stay true to yourself.

When you remember your mission to inspire others, it will give rise to courage to make the impossible possible."

Jeena Earthiva,

Belgium

Jenna@consciousmusiccode.com

38. *"Life has taught me that walking by faith and trusting God is the greatest way to live.*

When you trust God, it doesn't matter what obstacles come your way — you keep your eyes on the prize and keep moving forward. In time, everything begins to shift in your favor. Success is not just a destination; it's a way of being, a lifestyle anchored in faith and perseverance.

If I could speak to my younger self, I would say:

'God loves you more than you could ever imagine. You have been chosen. Trust His plan, because He is going to bless you beyond anything you can dream — not just for yourself, but so you can be a blessing to others.'"

Lima Maclean

New Jersey, USA

limam@jnaconsult.com

39. *"When you're calm, you're more focused, your decision-making improves, and your confidence rises.*

My favourite calming technique: Inhale deeply, hold for a few seconds, exhale slowly, as if blowing through a straw."

Micheline Trottier,

Onatario, Canada

Info@michelinetrottier.com

40. *"Above and beyond all else you must strive to TRULY and SINCERELY know your self first. For tomorrow never knows who you are TRULY and SINCERELY meant to be."*

Dan Alice

Ontario, Canada

519 259 9091

41. *"Be kind to yourself; even on the days you feel lost, you are growing through what you cannot yet see.*

Your story is unfolding into a life more beautiful than you can imagine."

Bonnie Milletto

Oregon, USA

www.bonniemilletto.com

42. *"You were never meant to shrink to make others comfortable. BElieve in yourself — wildly, deeply, and unapologetically. Let go of needing approval. Release the heavy weight of self-doubt. You are not here to be small; you are here to be love in motion and strength wrapped in kindness. Stand tall in who you choose to BE. When you love yourself fiercely, you will never be alone — your own heart will always be your home."*

Vicki McDougall

Ontario, Canada

vicki@vmbeautiful.com

43. *"Be bold. Be fearless. Be the rebel your soul came here to be.*

Speak your truth with love, let it be your key.

Question the known, embrace the unknown.

No limits can hold you, no stars are too far.

You are the miracle, you are the star.

You are the one, my dear. Always have been. Always will be."

Alison Davis

New Zealand

www.alisondavisglows.com

44. "The moment you stop seeking validation outside of yourself is the moment you remember your own power. Your story was never about survival — it was about rising into the wholeness you already are. Every experience, even the painful ones, was elevating the strength, wisdom, and compassion you now carry into the life you're meant to build."

Candice K., Kelowna, British Columbia, Canada

@candiceknight717

45. *"Stay curious and compassionate. Regularly ask yourself why you're doing something. If it brings you joy, keep doing it; if it's driven by guilt or obligation, let it go. Embrace your individuality by honoring what feels right for you and discarding what no longer serves you"*

Worcester MA

Kerri Lewis

klou.grace@gmail.com

46. *"Know that life's journey may feel like it has mountains to climb and deep valleys you feel you may never get of. It all is a part of the journey and if you look at it the right way and stretch it the mountains and deep valleys become even making a straight line. The line GOD always saw; straight, to get you to the person you are meant to be."*

Jon Emery

United States

jonemery33@gmail.com

47. *"Always remember, you are enough just as you are. Embrace your sensitivity; it is your greatest gift. Your kindness, compassion, and empathy have a profound impact on those around you. Let your intuition guide you; it's your internal compass, lighting your path forward. Trust yourself completely—everything you need is already within you."*

Tammy Gagnier,

Ontario, Canada

gagnier.3@gmail.com

48. *"You got this!"*

Christopher Blackwell

Brisbane, Australia

chris@christopherblackwell.com.au

49. *"My advice to my younger self would be to embrace yourself. All the awkward, weird, uniqueness that makes you YOU. Stick with the feelings you feel, keep loving nature and the beauty of this world. Don't listen to those people telling you to be someone else."*

Amber Durbin,

Oklahoma, USA

amberbug67@yahoo.com

50. *"Sex should be about Love. Never sell sex via video or in- person = digital forever evidence & PTSD."*

Nattolie Chilton,

Alberta Canada

nattoliechilton@gmail.com

51. *"One day, you'll create a global movement called Healing Millions—a sacred mission to bring peace and healing to the world. At first, not everyone will understand. They may doubt you. But your vision wasn't given to them—it was given to you, for a reason. You have the courage. The heart. The fire. And when it gets hard, your purpose will carry you through. This dream was never too big for you. It was perfectly made for you. So rise. Speak it. Build it. Be brave. Shine your light—because the world needs the love and light inside you more than ever."*

Nina Maglic,

Born in Bosnia and Herzegovina, now living in Vienna, Austria

ninamaglic.com

52. *"Stop searching. You'll never find it. Turns out everything you need is within you.*

We are spiritual beings living this human experience. Take life as that- a ginormous experience. What a beautiful, wild, tragic, lovely, confusing ride.

Now listen… the only thing you need to do is be present. Connect with as many humans as possible. We don't get to decide who deserves love- because everybody does. You are love. Be unapologetically you- F*** what people think. Keep your intentions pure, have integrity, and buckle up. It's a ride of a lifetime."

Gabby LaPress

Rochester, NY

glapress10@gmail.com

716-866-7635

53. *"Suspend all doubt as if you have already come through the other side, knowing, not only will you survive the present challenge, you will elevate the lesson that was hidden within that challenge and be better for it!"*

Laura Brennan Ballet

USA

http://www.thescienceofempowerment.com/

54. *"If I could talk to my younger self, I would say that you are enough, you are valued, your voice matters, and there is nothing wrong with being shy. Be proud of who you are, and what others think doesn't matter, it's what you think and feel that is important."*

Laura Cross,

Fair Grove, Missouri.

www.whitesandsselfcare.com

55. *"I wish my younger self knew that asking for help is not a sign of weakness. My favourite expression is: It's no for sure unless you ask. People want to help you, just ask and be amazed at the opportunities that come your way."*

Cathy Nesbitt

Ontario, Canada

cathy@cathysclub.com

56. *"I'm only as good enough as I believe I am."*

Cindy Edington

Fairport, NY

https://tranquilheartwellness.com

57. *"You are not broken — you are becoming.*

Every challenge, every tear, every moment you felt too much or not enough was shaping you into the healer, guide, and light you were born to be. Your sensitivity is your superpower. Trust your inner voice — she already knows the way home."

With love,"

Lynda –

Salt Lake City, Utah

lbarrus2@icloud.com

58. *"Don't let society's idea of beauty make you not see your own beauty."*

Tammy Williams

Ontario, Canada

tammy@womenchampagneandrealestate.com

59. *"Hope is never lost, there is life after loss. We often think that there is no way to heal but we start to heal when we can remember our loved ones with more love than pain. Always go where love is, that's where life is."*

Marie Bailey

Ontario, Canada

mariegidge1@gmail.com

60. *"Your intuition is far more powerful than you think. Your mind, and your heart, will sometimes get in the way, and muddy up what you KNOW. Always trust that first knowing!!!"*

Kristie Nantais

Ontario, Canada

Intacthealing@gmail.com

61. *"Above all, be kind. Be kind to others and to yourself. Take the time to truly listen, and then listen a little more; people don't always need answers, just understanding. Lean on your family and friends, including your colleagues, because community is strength. Lead by example with humility, empathy, and calmness, even in challenging moments. Finally, do not forget to laugh, and laugh often. Joy connects us, heals us, and reminds us what really matters."*

Beth Adlam,

Ontario, Canada

e_adlam@hotmail.com

62. *"You were born with God given Intuition, an inner knowing if something feels good or not.*

Hone your awareness of it, listen to it, let it guide your decisions, trust it, for it will never lie, and it may just save your life. Stay true to who you are and never succumb to other people's opinions, they're not walking in your shoes"

Mandy E. Robinson

Ontario Canada

freedm49@gmail.com

63. *"Every night before you go to bed, say the following:*

I forgive everyone.

Everyone forgives me.

May we all live in love and peace.

May we all know our lives have deep meaning and great purpose.

Let us all swing the doors open

To infinite joy, happiness, and prosperity."

Dr. Beverly Wixon

Florida, USA

beverly@beverlywixon.com

64. *"In the course of your awakening, your soul will die a thousand deaths, drawing you deeper into your innermost self. A place where light is forged out of the darkness of your own unhealed wounds. It is here, in this inner sanctuary of your own divine essence, that your soul will rise as it cries the tears of a thousand lifetimes, finally giving voice to the pain that wasn't allowed to speak. In that moment, you will understand the depths of your own power and the freedom that your voice will not only give yourself but also give others."*

Stacy-Lyn Corlett

Ontario, Canada

stacy-lyncorlett@soulfulwellnesssolutions.com

65. *"Don't only forgive those who may have hurt you in a life lesson. But also thank them for that lesson and move on. Don't look back! Just learn, live, and love yourself before others. No one else is here to save you or love you the way only you truly can."*

Halley-Rose

519-564-9211

66. *"It is none of my business what you are doing in your life. It is only my business what I do in my life! Make sure your cup is full and overflowing before giving to others. Only then can you help others wholeheartedly! Remember to never dull your light!"*

Elif Leung

Ontario, Canada

Elifiedinc@gmail.com

67. *"Embrace yourself. All the awkward, weird, uniqueness that makes you YOU. Stick with the feelings you feel, keep loving nature and the beauty of this world. Don't listen to those people telling you to be someone else."*

Amber Durbin,

Stillwater, Oklahoma.

68. *"Follow the passion that lights you up — it's the compass of your soul. The dreams that stir your heart were placed there for a reason. Trust them. Even when the path feels uncertain, passion will always illuminate the next step. Your soul already knows the way; you simply have to say yes."*

Edyta France, n.d.

Ontario, Canada

www.AscendNow.ca

69. *"When you're calm, you're more focused, your decision-making improves, and your confidence rises.*

My favourite calming technique: Inhale deeply, hold for a few seconds, exhale slowly, as if blowing through a straw. Repeat"

Ontario, Canada

Micheline Trottier

Info@michelinetrottier.com

70. *"When you chase your dreams, don't just be the dog that catches the car—be the smart puppy who already knows how to drive it. Manifestation isn't just about calling it in; it's about becoming the person who effortlessly embodies your vision. Step fully into the "YOU" you need to BE, and watch your dreams chase you instead."*

Carole Filion

Ontario Canada

647-273-5531

71. *"Happiness isn't something you find — it's something you design, one intentional choice at a time. Care for your Health, hold Affection for yourself, live with Purpose, build strong Partnerships, and stay Youthful at heart. Life will shatter and rebuild you, and please remember, you are always evolving into something stronger."*

Leigh Ann Hello

Ontario, Canada

www.HelloHappiness.ca

72. *"My advice to women in pursuit of excellence is to train yourself to receive and rest well so you don't dim your essence or withhold your truest and best from the people you love and your purpose.*

Practice receiving without Big Pride that says, "I don't need it," or Little Pride that says, "I don't deserve it." Practice resting without Guilt or Shame, saying, "I need to do more" or "I should." It will require discipline rooted in deep love, and when you move in that freedom, your power is channeled and replenished, and you will find fulfillment."

Samantha Stewartz

Pennsylvania, USA

stewartzsamantha@gmail.com

73. *"Your intensity isn't too much—it's insight. Your tears weren't weakness—they were training. You're not dramatic. You're discerning."*

Raquel Soto

Chicago, USA

https://yourgpsforsuccess.net/

74. *"Advice to younger self....Spend more time with mom & dad, listen and ask about family history.*

Go to more family functions instead of putting in extra hours on the business.

Do your work, but enjoy your family, they won't always be here.

Make sure you take care of yourself so you can live a long and productive life.

Spend time with your loved ones sharing stories and having fun.

Every day is a Gift, cherish the day and live in the now."

Michael Crawley

Ontario, Canada

michael@theprofessorofprosperity.com

75. *"You don't have to earn your worth, it's already woven into your being. Stop shrinking to make others comfortable; your light was never meant to be dimmed. Be patient with your process, but fierce with your boundaries. Say yes to yourself more than you say yes to others. Outgrowing people and places isn't loss, it's growth. Stop waiting for permission to be powerful. You are not here to be liked by others, you are here to be whole. You don't need to fix, prove, or perform to be enough. Walk away from what costs your peace, and stay anchored in your truth. Every time you choose yourself, you reclaim your freedom. This is your life. Own it—loudly, proudly, unapologetically."*

Soné Swanepoel

Cape Town, South Africa

soneswanepoel.com

76. *"Leading with love means approaching every situation with compassion and empathy, fostering connections that inspire trust and collaboration. By dropping from your head to your heart, you embrace vulnerability and authenticity, allowing deeper understanding and emotional resonance in your interactions."*

Jenny Natyshak

Ontario, Canada

Leadingwithloveltd@gmail.com

77. *"Remember ...Relaxed Breathing + slight smile + muscle relaxation= Calm Nervous System*

Calm nervous system supports the healing state. Connecting to your inner light and Higher Power can make a difference. Don't give up. Keep believing."

LoriKay Coleman

Gilbert, Az

enlightenedlifepath@gmail.com

78. *"The day you plant the seed is not the day you eat the fruit. Be patient and keep watering it."*

Dr. Mel Gill

Elmhurst, Illinois

79. *"When we're faced with challenges and feeling devastatingly overwhelmed, or paralyzingly stuck, that we slow down, and take a moment to realize, if we progressively make things "Emotionally Manageable," you will find nothing is impossible!"*

Founder of JEKL

James C. Brennan

80. *"The deepest wounds often hold the greatest wisdom. Allow yourself to feel, heal, and rise from your struggles, for it is in embracing your darkness that you'll discover the light within."*

Jane Cordeiro

Ontario, Canada

JaneCordeiro76@hotmail.com

81. *"Life is all about choices, so never say never! Learn the importance of wanting vs needing something."*

Deb Duncan

Ontario, Canada

82. *"We are truly only here to love one another and not necessarily in a romantic way!! No one is better than another person, we are all here for the same purpose!!"*

Leza Kjarsgaard

Ontario, Canada

Klezak@hotmail.com

83. *"Have a vision, believe in yourself, take massive action, be coachable, and accountable"*

Saraiki Abungwo

UK

info@blesatech.co.uk

84. *"Never let negative people make you believe that your dreams are impossible. Just start! Go for it!"*

Szabó Bianka Anna

Hungary

beecorpszerkesztoseg@gmail.com

85. *"Your life will be a roller coaster of extreme high's and rock bottom lows. Hold on with both hands, don't close your eyes or you could miss a lesson you will need later. Love yourself first and foremost, but not through your ego. Eat fresh, drink water, meditate daily, exercise regularly in the sun, enjoy everything you do. You are destined for gentle greatness, prepare well my friend."*

Louise Size

Australia

Louise.Size@gmail.com

86. *"People will flow through your life. The ones you love the most will never leave you even when they die. Let those who love you the most flow alongside you without grasping onto them. Let those who are meant to flow in and out give their gifts and flow on. You are always the one who will be there for you from cradle to grave so love yourself deeply. Health is wealth"*

Gayla D'Gaia

Gayladgaia@gmail.com

87. *"Stop trying to squeeze your big, bold life into jeans that were never made for your kind of magic. You were never meant to be 'one size fits all.' Your dreams? High-waisted. Your voice? Bootcut bold. Your worth? Stretchy, timeless, and never out of style. You'll spend too many years trying to fit in—at work, in rooms, in relationships. Spoiler alert: You're not meant to fit in. You're meant to break the mold and rock your own damn style. (Also, jeans with actual pockets = non-negotiable by 40.) Wear what fits your soul, not just your hips. And remember—midlife isn't a crisis, it's your comeback tour. Strut on, Your Future Self—now living in jeans with room to breathe*
▌⁺˟ Love, Your Wiser, Wilder Self. By My Darling."

Anjana Lala

South Africa, Johannesburg

hello@anjanalala.com

88. *"You are not behind—you are exactly where you're meant to be. Trust the timing of your life, and stop dimming your light to make others comfortable. Every challenge is shaping your brilliance, so lean into the fear, take the leap, and never forget: you were born to rewrite the rules and lead with love."*

Luc Gill

New York, Chicago and Singapore

Lucgill@gmail.com

89. *"Find out what makes your heart sing — then do a lot of it. Don't wait for permission. NEVER shrink to fit. Shine as bright as you can. The more you live what you love, the more the magic unfolds around you. That's how life begins to dance with you. YOU are the dancer. YOU are truly a divine piece of art. And now, go out and play!"*

Lucie Lynch,

Germany

lucie@lucielynchmusic.com

90. "Whether the lesson is good or bad, always ask yourself, "What did I learn from it?"

Nicole Harvick

South Carolina USA

nicoleharvick@gmail.com

91. *"You are perfect just the way you are right now. Every little part of you. Every aspect. Every quality. Your appearance. The way you think is so beautiful. No matter what you're going through, you are worthy of your Wholeness, of your vulnerability, of your kind of Love, and of your Inner Peace."*

Kelly Spinarsky,

Ontario, Canada

kellyspinarsky@gmail.com

92. *"Be yourself! Love yourself. Embrace your flaws! Worry less about what others think of you! Have goals but don't forget to live in the moment Be kind to others but remember you deserve respect and compassion too. Surround yourself with people who bring out your sparkle and your gifts! Dance like no one is watching!"*

Heather Shanahan

Maidstone, Ontario, Canada

93. *"Walk with confidence and command respect from others. You deserve it. You are strong, intelligent, and beautiful. You are a gift. You are going places. Stand tall. Make them work for it. Eat clean and green and avoid toxins. Your future health depends on it."*

Julie A Diaz

New Jersey, United States

Coachjulie6@yahoo.com

94. *"To love yourself, to forgive yourself and to believe in yourself. You are a worthy and important soul to the world."*

Theresa Bornais

Ottawa, Canada

tbornais@yahoo.com

95. *"Trust the path you're on—your spark began with witnessing your parents' resilience and will grow into a lifelong passion for care, advocacy, and transformation.*

Say yes to the hard roles; they'll shape your leadership and teach you to listen deeply, speak bravely, and act with integrity.

Have the courage to challenge what isn't right, even when your voice shakes, and know that systems change because people like you ask, "How can we do better?"

Be kind to yourself, seek mentors, rest when needed, and believe in the ripple effect of your voice—it's stronger than you know."

Wendy Trevarthen

Brisbane, Queensland, Australia

96. *"Keep your plans to yourself. Keep learning and doing the necessary. Be your own cheerleader, and celebrate every progress."*

Sanni Tju

Australia

sandiju7981@gmail.com

97. *"Be who you want to be. Don't be someone else to impress others. My life goal is to strive to make a difference in every life I touch."*

Dianne St. John

Ontario, Canada

98. *"My Advice to my younger self: If you want to learn how to never be manipulated or hurt by those who never deserved your love to begin with, learn to use your pain into power by reclaiming those haunting memories into your battle scars that proved that you won the war."*

Domina Rose,

Rancho Cucamonga, CA

fearlessfemme.defense@gmail.com

99. *"Be happy where you are...."*

M Cam

Ontario, Canada

laserkayakgirl@gmail.com

100. *"Ask, listen and listen to advice"*

Marilynn Guilbeault

Ontario, Canada

101. *"I wish I had been taught how to meditate daily when I was young. Contemplation and focus change everything."*

David Broad

Ontario, Canada

reikiwindsor@gmail.com

102. *"Take the time to meditate regularly, have more fulfilling relationships with others and keep up with racquet sports. I wish I had discovered pickleball much earlier in retirement, it gave me new energy, new health, many new people and new life drive."*

Dan Alice

Ontario, Canada

103. *"Nurture my friendships and always make time for my girlfriends. When relationships and life fall apart, your friends will be the ones you lean on. They will be there to celebrate when life is good and lift you when it isn't. You can't put a price on lifelong friends and the value they will bring to your life."*

Brieanna Beneteau

Ontario, Canada

beneteau.bm@gmail.com

104. *"Don't worry so much. Most of the bad things you think may happen never actually do."*

Andrea O'Neil

Ontario, Canada

105. *"Don't let society's idea of beauty make you not see your own beauty.?"*

Tammy Williams

Toronto, Ontario

tammy@womenchampagneandrealestate.com

106. *"My advice to women in pursuit of excellence is to train yourself to receive and rest well so you don't dim your essence or withhold your truest and best from the people you love and your purpose.*

Practice receiving without Big Pride that says "I don't need it" or Little Pride that says, "I don't deserve it." Practice resting without Guilt or Shame saying, "I need to do more" or "I should." It will require discipline rooted in deep love and when you move in that freedom, your power is channeled and replenished and you will find fulfillment."

Samantha Stewartz

Pennsylvania, USA

stewartzsamantha@gmail.com

107. *"Prioritize Self Discovery"*

Angie Petersen Green

Born Nebraska. Currently Oklahoma

sacredtransitiondoula@gmail.com

108. *"Get out of your head and pay attention. The world is always telling you everything you need to know."*

Céleste Desmarais

Ontario, Canada

celestescafe777@outlook.com

109. *"Be grateful for the people who hurt you. They can serve as a character in your next book, where you win every time."*

Portia Booker,

Ohio, USA

talktome@groovewithportia.com

110. *"You don't need to shrink yourself to be loved. The right people will never be intimidated by your fire, your vision, or your softness. They won't mistake your vulnerability or your flaws for weakness— they'll see them as proof that you're real. Your love is powerful. Your voice is worthy. And your dreams? They're not unrealistic. They are divine whispers of who you're becoming— and who you've always been, deep down."*

Stephanie C Vang

Saint Paul, Minnesota

steph@windgardenbooks.com

111. *"Always trust your gut. That quiet voice, that nudge, that feeling deep in the pit of your stomach — it's there to guide you. Whether it's heightening your senses, telling you when enough is enough, or gently asking you to pause and be still — listen. Your intuition is your protector, your compass, and your deepest truth. She knows the way."*

Jennifer Rogers

Oklahoma-US

jennifer@ukiyowellness.com

Christa Rose

Christa Rose | Speaker · Author · Mentor · Healer

Christa Rose is a four-time Amazon #1 bestselling author, international speaker, TV-Cohost, and certified coach who helps people cut through confusion and reconnect with purpose. Her journey — from a traumatic childhood, a devastating car accident, addiction, and widowhood at 24, to battling a chronic illness — shaped her into a powerful voice for resilience, healing, and transformation.

Her Amazon #1 Bestselling book *Skip the Pain, Experience the Pleasure* and collaborative books have touched lives worldwide. Christa Rose, author of *Shattering Truths I Wish My Younger Self Knew*, created a global movement around this exact message—truths that spark deep awareness and life-changing ah-ha moments, the kind that ultimately set you free.

With expertise in nutrition, healthcare leadership, and certifications in coaching, energy healing, Reiki Master and natural medicine, intuitive readings as well as other modalities, Christa blends practical wisdom with deep spiritual insight. She's been featured on TV, podcasts, and global magazines, and is known for her ability to meet people exactly where they are because she's been there offering a rare opportunity to provide clarity, insights and actionable steps.

Whether speaking at retreats, corporate events, or community gatherings, Christa leaves audiences inspired and ready to take aligned action long after the lights go out. Her mission: to inspire, give hope, and help others live not just a life they like — but one they love.

SIGNATURE TOPICS

✓ **W.A.I.T**
What Am I Thinking
Why Am I Talking
What Actions I'm Taking
=Your Reality
✓ Intentional Living

✓ Breaking the Burnout Cycle:
The Holistic Way to Restore, Recharge, and Reignite
✓ Grieving the Life You Thought You'd Have
✓ Will Tailor Any Speech For You

LET'S WORK TOGETHER!

I'm happy to answer any questions or hear anything you'd like to share

 messagechrista@gmail.com

christarose.com

About the Author

Christa grew up in Ontario, Canada — but life didn't exactly hand her a smooth ride. From an unstable childhood to surviving a brutal head-on collision, she faced more by her mid-20s than many do in a lifetime. Addiction followed, and at just 24, she was a widow and single mom. Years later, her journey took another turn when she was diagnosed with a rare, chronic illness that changed everything.

But Christa doesn't just survive — she transforms.

Her story, shared in poems and featured in other books, has lit a spark in readers searching for hope in the middle of heartbreak. After being encouraged countless times to tell her full story, she wrote *Skip the Pain, Experience the Pleasure: Cut the Crap That's Holding You Back So You Can Live the Life You Love!* It quickly became a **four-time Amazon #1 Bestseller** and **six-time #1 Hot New Release**. It's a fast, funny, and powerful read that's found its way into book clubs around the world — delivering perspective-shifting insight, and often, a much-needed laugh.

Christa didn't stop there. She co-authored **several other Amazon #1 bestselling books**, each one packed with real stories and wisdom that continue to make an impact in people's lives around the world.

Then came her next calling: *Shattering Truths I Wish My Younger Self Knew.* She opened up **111 free spots** for people across the globe to share life-changing advice — not just for their younger selves, but for anyone who might pick up the book. It's become more than advice you would give your younger self — it's a movement of healing, truth, and human connection.

Her career has always centered around service. Christa worked for nearly a decade as a **Nutrition Manager** in hospitals before helping open two long-term care homes — stepping into the role of **Director**. Her passion for helping others only grew, leading her to become a **Certified Coach Practitioner**, **Leadership Coach**, **Mindset Strategist**, and a **Mentor** whether it be spiritually based, insight on how to write their own book or discover their own unique gifts and talents to help themselves and others. With a strong intuitive gift, she helps people who lack clarity, direction and confidence cut through confusion, reconnect with their purpose, and create a life that feels truly aligned.

Her own health journey deepened her understanding of resilience. After battling Lyme disease and fibromyalgia, she developed mysterious symptoms: seizures, paralysis, loss of speech and eyesight, and unrelenting pain. It took three grueling years before she was diagnosed with **Anti-GAD65**, a rare autoimmune disease. When conventional medicine wasn't enough, Christa turned to **energy healing**, and it was there that true recovery began. Today, she shares her story to raise awareness of rare illnesses that too often go unseen and misdiagnosed.

People often call her an **Earth Angel** — not because she has all the answers, but because she shows up right when people need her, offering comfort, clarity, and sometimes the exact message they didn't even know they were looking for.

Christa's healing path includes certifications in **Reiki**, **The Radiance Technique®**, **Reiki Master**, **Energy Conscious Bars**, **Reflexology**, **Emotional Freedom Techniques** (**EFT**) continued her studies in **Natural Medicine and Herbalism**, as well as becoming a **Certified Sacred Freedom Technique Practitioner**. She's also a gifted **Akashic Record reader**, **tea-leaf reader**, and **card reader**. But more than the modalities, it's her ability to *really see people* — and connect with them on a much deeper level that makes all interactions so powerful.

She's been featured on podcasts, and interviews including being a TV Co-host that helped her reach more people globally. She's been highlighted in many magazines and articles including the cover story of Soul Of A Diamond global magazine.

Whether speaking on stages of all kinds, retreats, corporate events, or community gatherings, Christa's message is engaging, uplifting, and full of soul. She leaves every audience inspired and deeply moved with actionably skills, and more importantly, ready to take the next step in their own journey.

Her mission? To spread kindness, ignite inspiration, and offer hope — so others can not only live a life they like... but one they truly love.

Reviews: Shattering Truths I Wish My Younger Self Knew

"Christa's book is like sitting down with a wise, loving friend who holds your hand through the messy, beautiful, heartbreaking, and hopeful moments we all wish we could go back and do over. Each truth feels like a permission slip to let go of what no longer serves you and step boldly into the life you truly deserve. Christa's honesty, humor, and raw vulnerability cracked my heart open in the best way. This book is a gift for anyone who's ever felt lost, stuck, or too broken to begin again. It reminds you—gently but powerfully—that you are worthy, you are resilient, and you are never alone."

Nina Maglic, Austria

CEO of Healing Millions

"Shattering Truths I Wish My Younger Self Knew

A heartfelt mirror of resilience, wisdom, and emotional transformation. A Journey of Healing and Truth

As I pen this review, I imagine placing it gently in the hands of someone standing at the edge of self-doubt, perhaps that someone is you. This isn't just a book. It's a mirror. A letter. A friend. A guide; isn't here to fix you; it's here to remind you that you were never broken.

From the first tender line 'I wish I could go back in time and give you a big hug' to the final soul-stirring declaration of worth and unconditional love, this book speaks straight from the heart and lands softly into yours. Whether you're 16 or 60, the truths within these pages transcend age. They are as timeless as they are timely.

The author's voice is electric with honesty. There's humor ("ran into my ex at a gas station while wearing my worst outfit"), there's deep introspection, and there's a disarming refusal to sugarcoat. Yet, beneath every truth is hope that you can heal, shift, grow, and forgive. The recurring call to "WAIT What Am I Thinking?" is brilliant in its simplicity. It's the mental reset button most of us don't know we need.

What Makes This Book a Standout

1. Voice that Heals. There is a rawness in the writing that feels like a best friend finally saying the things you've longed to hear.

2. Universal Truths. Though framed as a letter to a younger self, the wisdom is evergreen. You don't outgrow this book; you grow with it.

3. Practical and Poetic. Balancing actionable advice with literary eloquence, the writing weaves science, soul, and storytelling into one powerful tapestry.

4. Relatable Realism. From missed highway exits to pizza guilt and sarcastic friends, the author makes emotional intelligence approachable.

'Shattering Truths I Wish My Younger Self Knew' Whether you're 16 or 60, these truths speak across time, offering both tender validation and an empowering nudge toward becoming the author of your own story."

The Legendary Coach Eve

Scotland

"This book is a fierce, soul-stirring journey that will *shatter* you in all the best ways. Christa shares her own shattering of old belief systems with unapologetic truth, weaving in wisdom, quotes, and bold action steps that push you to *really* see yourself. It's raw, real, and an absolute life reflection. This book is the permission slip your soul's been waiting for."

Jennifer Rogers

Oklahoma, USA

"Reading *Shattering Truths I Wish My Younger Self Knew* is like sitting with a wise, fun person who's walked through fire and kept their sparkle. Christa doesn't preach; she relates, reflects, and hands you the pen to author your next chapter.

I am getting a book for my friend and my daughter, because as I was pouring through the pages, I had all those ah-ha moments that were captivating, and some advice was practically life-changing!

If you're craving a hug wrapped in practical mindset tools you can both, *feel* and use this book as you pour yourself a latte, grab a highlighter, or just open to a random page and dive in. Your younger self (and your future clients) will thank you."

Tina Brigley, Entrepreneur and Personal Development Coach

Ontario, Canada